SUSTAINABLE MINIMALISM

SUSTAINABLE MINIMALISM

Embraze Zero Waste, Build Sustainability Habits That Last,
and Become a Minimalist without Sacrificing the Planet

Stephanie Marie Seferian

mango

PUBLISHING GROUP

CORAL GABLES

Cover Design: Elina Diaz
Cover Photo/illustration: Salih/stock.adobe.com
Layout & Design: Elina Diaz

For permission requests, please contact the publisher at:
Mango Publishing Group
2850 S Douglas Road, 2nd Floor
Coral Gables, FL 33134 USA
info@mangopublishinggroup.com

For special orders, quantity sales, course adoptions and corporate sales, please email the publisher at sales@mango.bz. For trade and wholesale sales, please contact Ingram Publisher Services at customer.service@ingramcontent.com or +1.800.509.4887.

Sustainable Minimalism: Embrace Zero Waste, Build Sustainability Habits That Last, and Become a Minimalist without Sacrificing the Planet

Library of Congress Cataloging-in-Publication number:
ISBN: (print) 978-1-64250-501-6 , (ebook) 978-1-64250-502-3
BISAC category code: HOM019000—HOUSE & HOME / Cleaning, Caretaking & Organizing

Printed in the United States of America

To Haig, Ani, and Lara

Table of Contents

The Sustainable Minimalist Tree
Work Your Way to the Top!

PART 3

Community
- Share resources
- Prioritize small, local businesses
- Rely on the gift economy

Advocacy
- Lead with inclusivity
- Encourage fact-based discussions
- Be solutions-oriented

PART 2

Family Values
- Replace single-use plastic
- Reduce carbon footprint
- Revive age-old skills

Household Products
- Go non-toxic
- Embrace homemade
- Focus on eco-friendly

Health & Beauty
- Simplify beauty routine
- Experiment with all-natural
- Focus on holistic

PART 1

Home
- Tidy up
- Get organized
- Become waste-conscious

Finances
- Eliminate unnecessary expenses
- Streamline (and stick to!) budget
- Commit to intentional purchasing

Travel
- Fly less
- Drive less
- Purchase carbon offsets

The 5 Guiding Principles

1. Intentional simplicity
2. Conscious consumerism
3. Sustainability
4. Self-sufficiency
5. Advocacy

Introduction

America, we have a purchasing problem.

I'll never forget the first (and only) time I participated in Black Friday. I woke up early—too early, if I'm honest—and stood in a line that snaked around the side of a big box store. It was a frigid November night and I shuffled from side to side to keep warm. The lights in the parking lot illuminated the exhalations of the crowd; in that moment, I had the fleeting thought that *this* was all so silly. I should go home. I should get back in bed.

But in the end, I bought a flat screen television. I saved some money, but not all that much. The TV worked, but only for a few years before it pixelated and on-screen images became unrecognizable. When I look back on this particular Black Friday, I realize I was right: I should have gone home. I wish I had gone back to bed.

Corporations want us to believe that happiness lies in stuff, but research suggests otherwise. In 2018, 40 percent of Americans said they were more anxious than the year prior,[1] and one in fifteen reported symptoms of depression.[2] Our buying behavior has catapulted us into debt—the average American has four credit cards and a collective balance of $6,200 at any given time.[3]

And what about our trash? While many consumers are in the habit of donating working items to make room for newer, shinier models, the vast majority of our perfectly working and perfectly fine discards find their ways into landfills.

Minimalism—the intentional choice to live with less—provides hope to overworked, overstressed, and overspent Americans. Adopters of a "less is more" lifestyle attest that minimalism offers the precious gifts of free time, mental clarity, and financial stability. But there is another, bigger benefit to living with less that no one is talking about: minimalism is key to saving our planet.

Although the minimalist lifestyle has experienced a rebirth in recent years, the concept is not new. Minimalism is mentioned in countless ancient texts; Buddhists have shunned material possessions for thousands of years. Yet twenty-first century minimalism is novel in that, these days, the concept of minimalism is entangled with the concept of decluttering. Modern minimalist influencers—including authors, social media personalities, and documentary stars—advocate for decluttering, yet remain silent on sustainability. As a result, aspiring minimalists in need of guidance find themselves on an endless hamster wheel of buying, decluttering, buying more, and purging again. From a historical perspective, overemphasizing decluttering and underemphasizing the reasons *why* we overbuy in the first place are thoroughly inconsistent with minimalism's purpose. This practice also steals Earth's resources, and for no good reason.

I found myself intrigued by minimalism shortly after becoming a mother, and for purely selfish reasons. My husband, Haig, and I—together with our dog and two cats—happily coexisted in an 850-square-foot apartment. But after our first daughter, Ani, was born, friends and family showered her with gifts. The sudden influx of baby toys, gear, and clothes slowly squeezed us out of our home.

Organizing, sorting, managing, and cleaning my daughter's seemingly infinite possessions ate away at rare moments of free time. My anxiety skyrocketed. I found myself asking big questions about the true costs of consumerism as I folded unworn outfits and scoured the apartment for places to store unused plastic toys. Although Western culture emphasizes having more was preferable to having less, I found myself questioning such logic. I daydreamed about what a simpler, greener way of living in the twenty-first century could look like. I wondered whether such an existence was even possible.

If I wanted to find peace within my own home, I needed to make a change. So I sought out camaraderie on the internet and lurked in a handful of minimalism groups. Minimalism no longer felt like an obscure, countercultural concept; after all, thousands of people just like me believed that less could mean more.

But that feel-good internet kinship faded with time. I couldn't cheer on fellow minimalists who photographed garbage bags full of recently decluttered, yet perfectly good possessions on the curb, awaiting trash pickup. I bristled at the idea that minimalism had to come at the expense of the planet. If minimalism was synonymous with unsustainable decluttering, I *wasn't* a minimalist.

So what was I, then? An environmentalist? To find out, I joined zero-waste groups. Whereas I received motivation from the minimalist groups, I received an education from the zero-waste ones. I learned exactly how our collective purchasing problem impacts the planet. I realized (to my horror) that climate scientists argue that irreversible changes to Earth's climate systems have been underway. I learned the real problems associated with plastic, and found the confidence to tackle my oversized carbon footprint head-on.

Living better means living with less.
But there, too, something didn't quite jive. Conversations within these communities so often felt either black or white, and eco-leaning behaviors were either right or wrong. There was also the ever-present contention between keeping stuff versus letting it go: while an environmentalist would theoretically keep everything in hopes of later reuse, a minimalist desired to let unused possessions go. I wanted to let items go!

I soul-searched. I understood intuitively that both minimalism and eco-friendliness are rooted in reduction. Owning less, needing less, and desiring less—the tenets of a minimalist lifestyle—also happen to be effective ways to live more sustainably. I realized that eco-friendly living and minimalism fall on opposite sides of a singular spectrum. While some identify on one end of the spectrum as environmentalists and many others on the other side as minimalists, there is an entire area in the middle for people who aspire to minimize sustainably.

Sustainable minimalism, then, is a movement grounded in the idea that living better means living with less. It's about making *incremental* tweaks to our daily lives to help preserve the planet for our children.

What Is Sustainable Minimalism?

Sustainable minimalism is a countercultural and radical stand against consumerism. It is also about:

- Reducing consumption as a means of lowering carbon emissions

- Decluttering responsibly with the planet in mind

- Refusing single-use products

- Recycling as a last resort

- Rethinking the status quo

- Strengthening local economies by buying locally

- Lowering environmental toxins

- Harnessing the power of hundreds and thousands of individuals doing their part

- Embracing self-sufficiency as the ultimate goal

How This Book Is Organized

Have you ever gone apple picking? Here in New England, where I live, apple picking is a must-do activity every autumn. It's a feel-good outing for the whole family precisely because everyone experiences success. Lara, my preschooler, snatches apples from the bottom branches while Haig and I pick from the middle of the tree. And my six-year-old? Ever the daredevil, Ani grabs the ladder, climbs to the highest wrung, and picks the untouched fruit at the top.

This book references a metaphorical apple tree to help you pivot from consumerist culture toward a slower, more intentional existence, because when you attempt to adopt a new lifestyle, it's prudent to be incremental. It's smartest to pick the apples toward the bottom of the tree first, and easiest, too.

In part 1 you will tackle the low-hanging fruit, decluttering responsibly and garnering an understanding of why people overbuy in the first place.

In part 2 you will build on your successes and address the middle of the tree. Here, you will create foundations that facilitate sustainable behaviors for the long term.

Finally, in part 3 you will foster minimalist self-sufficiency as a means of relying less on corporations and more on your own skills. Said another way, you have picked the rest of tree. Now it's time to grab the ladder.

Back when I started my soul-searching journey as a new mother, I couldn't find a community that supported my eco-friendly, minimalist ideals. I yearned for a space where like-minded parents could attain both camaraderie and concrete tips to live simpler lives, but back then, that space did not exist. So one day, while Lara napped, I bought a domain name without giving it much forethought. To this day, MamaMinimalist.com houses my blog and *The Sustainable Minimalists* podcast. With this book, as well as with my website and podcast, I hope to create a community that supports other aspiring sustainable minimalists.

Happy reading!

PART 1

Getting Started with the Low-Hanging Fruit

CHAPTER 1

Why You Overbuy (and How to Stop)

Capitalism Demands Consumers

Have you bought into the notion that possessions will make you happy? Do you confuse what you own with what you are worth? If so, you aren't alone.

An abundance of possessions is a symptom of affluent individuals and societies, and citizens of developed countries are indeed affluent. Between 1967 and 2017, the amount Americans spent annually increased nearly twenty-fold.[4] [5] The average American resides in a supersized home, has a different outfit for every day of the month, and has over 300,000 possessions.[6]

Multi-million dollar businesses have popped up to help you manage your stuff. Unsurprisingly, even though the size of the average American home has tripled in the last fifty years,[7] many own more than they can store. The self-storage and junk

Donation centers have an abundance of quantity and a severe lack of quality.

removal industries benefit from consumers who overbuy, and because aging citizens have accumulated possessions over their lifetimes, transition service companies have emerged to aid in the downsizing process. The business of downsizing is similar to the businesses of storage and removal: both profit from your emotional attachment to things.

For many, the decluttering process is both technically challenging and emotionally overwhelming. And while you may have lofty intentions of giving your unwanted items away to others in need, the vast majority of your discarded possessions will sit in donation centers. Donation centers have an abundance of quantity and a severe lack of quality, and while select clothing may be sold to rag dealers and outdated electronics may be scrapped for parts, the reality is that the majority of your possessions are likely to be viewed as junk. As such, they have nowhere to go except to the landfill.

There *is* hope: stopping the cycle starts with understanding it first.

Why You Overbuy

Never before in human history has it been easier to buy. You *can* buy, and so you likely do.

Both online retailers and brick-and-mortar store managers know that if they lower barriers to purchasing, you will buy

Overconsumption is a staple of Western culture and a consequence of collective wealth.

more than you intended. And while e-commerce boasts saved shipping and billing information during online checkout, brick-and-mortar stores churn out coupons, sales, and reward dollars to entice you inside, where they then expertly curate your shopping experience with familiar music, calming colors, and pleasant scents.

There are also personal factors at play when you purchase, including the following:

1. You're An Aspirational Shopper

If you are like most modern consumers, you buy not because you dream of owning something, but because you aspire to *be* someone. Your purchases are powerful statements about who you are and what you value: while an organic cotton T-shirt conveys ethics, a Louis Vuitton bag signals wealth and style. Your identity is intricately tied to your possessions, and aspirational purchasing may one way you attempt to become the best version of who you want to be.

Aspirational shopping is particularly prevalent among eco-conscious consumers who desire to improve the world with their dollars. Do you believe you have a responsibility to purchase products for the good of the planet? The smartest "green" brands lead consumers to believe that purchasing their products is part of a collective, worldwide movement for good. As men and women become more aware of—and subsequently more empowered through—their buying power, the market for sustainable, ethical, and socially responsible products continues to grow.

Yet there is a major catch to aspirational spending: making luxury purchases to achieve a status that isn't aligned with your true identity will not make you feel more confident, as you might expect. Instead, aspirational purchases may increase feelings of insecurity.[8] Over time, such insecurities reduce purchasing satisfaction, so you'll find yourself further encouraged to buy as a means of maintaining inner equilibrium.

2. You Chase That Shopping High

Shopping rewards you with surges of happiness, and you have evolution to thank for it.

Centuries ago, when early humans were hunter-gatherers, hoarding food and other goods increased the odds of survival. The trajectory of evolution predisposed you to accumulation: endorphins are powerful rewards that urge repetition of endorphin-releasing behaviors. As you stand at a store's checkout counter and hand over payment or click "Buy Now" online, you likely experience a wave of dopamine-induced happiness. In order to extend this "shopping high," your ancient reward system urges you to repeat buying behaviors.

Because goods are cheap and the barriers to buying are so low, you can likely buy whatever you desire whenever you want it, and purchasing becomes less satisfying as a result. In order to experience that same level of endorphin-releasing euphoria, you must increasingly buy more and more.

3. The Diderot Effect Is Real

Denis Diderot was an eighteenth-century French philosopher[9] who was gifted a luxurious scarlet dressing gown.[10] At first, Diderot was thrilled. He adored the thick fabric's feel and appreciated its unique craftsmanship.

But very soon after, the glamorous robe highlighted the collective shabbiness of his other possessions. To remedy this, Diderot bought new items as replacements. He removed his old straw chair and purchased a new one made of Moroccan leather. He trashed his old desk and placed an expensive new writing table in its place. And the prints that hung on his walls? He swapped them out with more elegant ones.

Behavioral psychology defines the Diderot effect as the idea that obtaining a new possession creates a spiral of consumption that leads people to make unnecessary purchases.[11] You end up buying items your prior self never needed to feel fulfilled after obtaining something new.

I have experienced the Diderot effect firsthand. Soon after we moved into our first house, Haig and I embarked on a small renovation project to update our woefully drab powder room. I had assumed the renovation process would be mundane, but I quite enjoyed it. I found myself happily comparing dozens of gray hues at the paint store; countless tile options utterly swept me up, too. We exceeded our allotted budget by opting for crown molding, and when the project was complete, our renovated bathroom surpassed my wildest expectations.

Yet it wasn't long before I noticed a problem: the opulence of my new powder room exposed the mediocrity of the rest of my home. Our new bathroom, with its upgraded fixtures and modern decor, felt out of place on my ho-hum first floor. All of a sudden, I found the dining room's built-ins particularly aged, and the upstairs bathroom and its outdated tiling embarrassing.

Has obtaining a new possession ever enticed you to purchase more? That is the Diderot effect at work.

4. Ads Are Powerful

The first television station began broadcasting in 1928, and for the first thirteen years of its existence, television was advertisement-free. But ad-free programming came to an end on July 1, 1941, when the first commercial aired.[12]

Advertisements are quite convincing, and you're likely more susceptible to their power than you realize. Corporations expertly expose you to an ad over a specific medium and over a specific time period, because constant exposure to the same message renders you more inclined to purchase. Some estimates suggest the average American sees and hears 5,000 advertisements per day—a staggering 1.8 million per year.[13]

Corporations also profit from human vulnerability by curating advertisement experiences that amplify your deepest desires and expose your biggest insecurities. And while marketing teams employ many techniques to entice consumers, one of the most pervasive is perceived obsolescence: messaging that suggests your existing, perfectly fine possessions are not good *enough*. Perceived obsolescence urges you to buy new items to replace what you already have, which leads to a constant cycle of buying and decluttering over and over again.

Advertisements play on humans' natural instinct to compare and compete. Before commercials, consumers "kept up with the Joneses" by comparing their successes with those of others in their economic sphere, including their neighbors. But the dawn of television, commercials, and the internet drastically expanded Americans' frames of reference for comparing and competing; social media has further exposed how people in higher socioeconomic spheres live. Whether you desire a competition or not, you may find yourself competing with affluence far beyond your realistic financial reach. *Psychology Today* reports, "Competitiveness is a biological trait that co-evolved with the basic need for human survival,"[14] so while it isn't a fair competition, you may buy with the subconscious hope of competing with those who are wealthier than you.

Real Life Sustainable Minimalists

Realigning Actions with Priorities

I started on my sustainable minimalist journey just after returning from a trip to the Caribbean where I scuba dove for the first time. I was mesmerized by the coral reefs and marine life, and the experience opened my eyes to two conflicting realizations: while I wanted to continue to travel and see the world's beauty, I had just witnessed the effects of coral bleaching firsthand. I was at a crossroads—how could I travel without further contributing to the destruction of the environment?

First, I examined my budget. I was ashamed to realize that I had let lifestyle inflation creep into my life. There were my afternoon caffeine fixes, small indulgences to which I often treated myself, and plenty of shopping sprees I went on for secondhand books. I found myself making excuses for my poor decisions. I needed caffeine to get me through the workday, right? Without it, how would I be a good employee and progress in my career?

As I learned about sustainability, I realized that my Chai tea lattes cost more than the $3.75 I paid, as they added plastic pollution to the oceans I loved. And my book shopping habit led to a cluttered bedroom floor overflowing with stacks of dusty books. How had things gotten so out of hand? I had been so careful not to fall for the latest trends, and I rarely obsessed over the newest gadget. Yet without realizing it, I had become a mindless shopper and a slave to that short burst of dopamine.

Unfortunately, you don't have to be a shopaholic to be a mindless shopper, and my spending habits revealed that my immediate wants had taken precedence over their impact on the environment. I could no longer willingly contribute to global warming, plastic waste, and species extinction. For me, it came down to realigning my actions with my priorities.

SARAH M., Sustainable Minimalists group member

The Consequences of Overbuying

An Increased Mental Load

If you are reading this book, you may have already come to a crippling realization: owning more results in more to organize, track, maintain, and worry about. Your "mental load," or emotional labor, describes the total sum of responsibilities required for you to manage your household. Women tend to experience heavier mental loads than men, as the never-ending domestic juggling act of organizing, thinking, planning, and keeping a home afloat continues to be considered a woman's job.[15] While heavy mental loads are linked to feelings of distress, emptiness, and lowered life satisfaction,[16] buying less and owning less are powerful ways to improve your quality of life.

Financial Stress

Perhaps you have experienced financial stress as a result of your purchasing habits. If so, you have company. Excluding home mortgages, the average American carried $38,000 in personal debt in 2018.[17] And while the median household income in the United States in 2019 was $59,039, Americans are living beyond their means—nearly half of American households spend so much that they don't save any money at all.[18] Not surprisingly, debt and stress go hand in hand. If you struggle to pay your bills, you're more than twice as likely to experience mental health problems like depression and severe anxiety.[19] Financial stress is linked to physical ailments, too, including migraines, insomnia, and cardiovascular disease. Then there are the less tangible, but still significant, consequences of debt and stress on overall function: resentment, anger, and shame can wreak havoc on your marriage and family life if left unchecked.

Environmental Implications

Discarded possessions emit methane into the atmosphere and produce leachate as they decompose in landfills.

The environmental implications associated with overbuying are many. All purchases—even the eco-friendly ones—contribute to environmental degradation because manufacturing demands nonrenewable resources, including fossil fuels like coal, crude oil, and natural gas.[20] When burned for manufacturing,

Out of sight does not mean out of planet. fossil fuels release carbon dioxide and other greenhouse gases into the air that warm our planet and contribute to climate change.[21]

While an item's creation is hardly environmentally benign, the effects of its afterlife are similarly concerning. Out of sight does not mean out of planet, and as discarded items decompose in landfills, they release methane, a powerful greenhouse gas.[22] They also produce leachate, a highly toxic, sludge-like liquid that is the byproduct of broken-down waste and water. Leachate pollutes soil and waterways in areas far beyond the dump.[23]

There's a solution to the personal and environmental consequences associated with overbuying, and it's actually quite simple: buy less.

Real Life Sustainable Minimalists

Why Organize Chaos?

I have always found shopping to be an enjoyable way to spend time with friends. As a kid, I'd spend my birthday money on the coolest new toy. When I was old enough to have a job, I scoured clearance racks with my friends for the cutest outfits. In early adulthood, I frequented home goods stores to find the perfect shower curtain or wall hanging for my apartment.

Fast-forward half a decade, my husband and I found ourselves in the midst of an international move. We watched as movers filled trucks with endless boxes. How had we accumulated so much stuff? Surely we didn't use or need everything we had jam-packed into those boxes. I looked around my new house and felt defeated. Where would I store all my gizmos and oddments? I stashed items here and there, but I knew I was simply organizing chaos.

This was my epiphany, and I ran with it. I purged. I made donation piles. While filling bags for thrift store drop off, I had three important realizations:

1. We rarely read a novel or watched a movie twice.
2. My clothes—which I purchased last season—already felt out of style.
3. Our home was cluttered with knickknacks, and I didn't like it.

I made small choices then, and I continue to make decisions every day as I continue on this path. Am I perfect? No. Do I still enjoy shopping with my friends? Absolutely, just more mindfully! I'm a woman on a mission to be better today than I was yesterday, for myself, my family, my home, and our planet.

ALLISON A., podcast listener

Your No-Spend Month

I was once a very self-centered consumer. In my twenties, I toiled as a teacher at a job I considered emotionally exhausting and attended graduate school in the evenings. I told myself that my life was hard (*it wasn't*) and that I deserved rewards (*I didn't*). And while I didn't necessarily characterize myself as a shopaholic, I *did* enjoy hunting for a good deal. I believed new outfits granted momentary reprieves from difficult workweeks, and thanks to dopamine-induced instant gratification, they often did. I had wholly accepted the notion that stuff creates happiness. Until I had children of my own, questioning this logic had never crossed my mind.

A practical first step toward adopting a lifestyle rooted in sustainable minimalism is to hop off the consumerist bandwagon, at least for a little while. A month-long shopping ban—also known as a no-spend month—provides an incremental opportunity to assess your spending habits.

After a particularly craze-inducing December, my family embarked on a No-Spend January. We found ourselves naturally desiring to stay home and hibernate, so to speak, and the challenge's parameters gifted my family both the opportunity and the freedom to recenter ourselves around one another. Haig and I spent more time with our children, especially as we pulled out forgotten toys and games from the basement. And on those Saturday afternoons when everyone felt antsy, we headed to the nearby children's museum—of which we are already members—instead of spending money on admission to kid-friendly attractions. The experience taught me a lesson I'd always known but forgotten: a slower pace just *feels* right.

The rules of a no-spend month are simple: spend on needs, save on wants. Continue to make payments toward essentials throughout the month, including bills, rent or mortgage, gas, and food, but restrict unnecessary purchases like clothing, dinners out, manicures, nonessential trips to the mall, and

any other spending opportunities that could reasonably be
considered frivolous.

---

5 Benefits of Shopping Bans

1. They allow you to get serious about your finances and
    perhaps meet a savings goal.

2. They reacquaint you with hobbies you have
    been neglecting.

3. They highlight the differences between wants
    versus needs.

4. They encourage you to slow down and spend quality
    time with loved ones.

5. They retrain your brain to desire less.

As you embark on your no-spend month, consider the
following pieces of advice:

Be Entertained

Whenever you seek entertainment or stimulation outside the
home (even a quick coffee date!), you almost inevitably end up
spending money. Open your home up to others by hosting a
board game tournament, inviting loved ones over for dinner,

or setting up the living room for a movie night with your best friends.

Hunker down with your immediate family, too, and find free ways to stay entertained. Embark on frequent hikes or bike rides, rewatch old DVD collections, pick up neglected hobbies, and check out video games, audio books, and eBooks from your local library.

Be Vocal

Don't keep it a secret: tell extended family and close friends what you're doing and why you're doing it. Empower your family and friends to offer you the support you need by making them aware of your no-spend goals. If you're secretive about your month's plans, you will find yourself in the awkward position of having to decline invitations and explain why after the fact.

Be Proactive

You will likely find yourself with excess free time during your no-spend month, so use it to unsubscribe from marketing lists. Doing so decreases the frequency with which you are exposed to advertisements and reduces unnecessary paper waste.

First, sign up for **Catalog Choice** (catalogchoice.org), a free service that unsubscribes you from junk mail. Next, make an account with **OptOutPrescreen.com** for yourself and other adults living in your house as a means of opting out of credit card offers. Use their online option, which is the easiest and fastest way to unenroll. Clean up your inbox spam, too, by signing up with **Unroll.Me**, a free app that quickly unsubscribes you from spam mailing lists. Finally, create an account with the **Data & Marketing Association**. Doing so will remove your address from the lists companies use to find new customers.

Be Decluttered

Many aspiring minimalists report that stepping back from consumerist culture gives them both the insight and the motivation to examine their existing possessions through a critical lens. Use the downtime your no-spend month offers to declutter your home once and for all. We will discuss exactly how sustainable minimalists declutter in the next chapter.

Common Concerns and How to Overcome Them

"I'm interested in participating in a no-spend month, but my spouse isn't on board. What do I do?"

First, sit down with your spouse and relay all the reasons why you'd like to try a no-spend month, and be sure to mention that your monthly savings will increase if everyone partakes in the challenge. If your spouse remains ambivalent, know you can still control your own spending, so feel confident knowing that you can embark on one by yourself.

"My mother's birthday falls during my spending moratorium. Should I just scratch the whole idea?"

Of course not! If there is a nonnegotiable event on your social calendar, go and enjoy yourself. Remember that sustainable minimalism is about progress, not perfection—good-faith efforts add up, and a single cheat day (or even two) won't singlehandedly destroy your momentum.

CHAPTER 2

The Five Pillars of Responsible Decluttering

Decluttered homes reduce stress, free up time, and provide clarity
for smarter purchasing decisions in the future.

One of the greatest compliments my home ever received came
from a friend who visited for a playdate: "Your house is always
so clean!"

I smiled, but shyly, because my home wasn't particularly clean that day. Clumps of dog hair lined the baseboards, my daughters had sprinkled the floor underneath the table with crumbly breakfast remnants, and fingertip smears ran the length of the sliding glass door. Yet my friend's compliment stayed with me after our playdate ended. Was my home actually cleaner than most, or was she commenting on something else entirely? And while my home certainly wasn't *clean*, it was devoid of clutter. Tidy spaces tend to feel more open, and decluttered homes often seem bigger. They appear cleaner, too, because having fewer possessions reduces visual overstimulation.

The Benefits of a Decluttered Home

Many adults—particularly mothers—attest that clutter creates anxiety, and evolutionary biology supports this experience. Order and symmetry gave our ancestors an advantage over predators, and humans therefore evolved to prefer tidy spaces.[24] And while you likely feel scattered and anxious when your living spaces are untidy, decluttering ensures that you are living in a calmer state, where it's easier to focus on what's important.

A minimalist home also reduces family tension. Maintaining tidiness maintains family harmony because it sets the foundation for an overall calmer internal baseline in adults.[25] Many adults attest that they despise being home because of the countless messes that demand their attention. Arguing

Clutter has a way of hiding what truly matters in plain sight, and clearing out the nonessentials ushers in clarity.

with your less-than-tidy spouse or snapping at your child for not picking up their toys unintentionally creates interpersonal stress. Paring down your belongings will likely encourage you to view your home as the antidote to stress instead of its cause. Decluttering may enable your partner and children to enjoy your best self, too, rather than your worst.

A decluttered home is much easier to maintain than a cluttered one. Americans spend an average of ninety minutes per day— or sixty hours per month—on household upkeep, including cleaning, tidying, and organizing.[26] But when you own less, you have fewer items to dust, wipe down, organize, and put away. As a result, you naturally have more time do what you love with the people you adore.

I consider decluttering to be a transformative event in the evolution of a sustainable minimalist. The purging process can be jarring—I myself felt profound shame as I stood over the piles of cheap junk I had mindlessly purchased. But that shame awakened me to an uncomfortable reality: I had bought many items I didn't need, and for no good reason. And while decluttering can absolutely be uncomfortable, it is an essential foundation for adopting a minimalist lifestyle. Clutter has a way of hiding what truly matters in plain sight, and clearing out the nonessentials ushers in clarity. When the job is done, you will likely realize you need much less than you thought to be happy.

Real Life Sustainable Minimalists

Organizing Isn't Enough

I first started decluttering when my daughter was a toddler. Although I have always been fairly organized, I had *a lot* of stuff. My organized clutter filled every available cupboard and closet in our home. Day after day, I spent time and energy picking up all the stuff my curious daughter got into. I quickly tired of wasting so much of my energy and patience picking up the same stuff, especially when it dawned on me that we didn't even use, need, or like most of it.

One day, I decided I had enough. I grabbed a laundry basket and walked around the house searching for anything we didn't use, need, or love. One basket turned into ten baskets. Still, I kept going.

Each time I began another round of decluttering, I was willing and able to let go of more and more. I realized I loved the benefits of living with less. I felt happier. Our home was tidier and more peaceful, which in turn helped me feel calmer. I had more time and energy when the stuff we owned wasn't taking up so much of them. I was more present and patient with my family, too. We even had more financial freedom as we focused less on buying and more on putting money toward our priorities.

It took several years and many rounds of decluttering to get to a point where I feel content with the amount of "stuff" we own. These days, I do a lot less decluttering and more maintaining, instead, because life isn't static—our needs and interests shift over time and the possessions we choose to own change along with them. I make sure every item we own has a designated place; I also make an effort to notice the things we no longer use, so clutter doesn't have a chance to build up again.

Over time, my simplifying journey has gone from decluttering our home to simplifying our lives as well. As a family, we aim to keep our schedule simple and clutter-free with plenty of white space to rest, recharge, and reconnect. Choosing to live with less has been such a wonderful way to live.

MELISSA RUSSELL, episode #061 podcast guest
simplelionheartlife.com

High-Impact Decluttering: Your Whole-House Plan

The following checklist outlines fifty-two commonly cluttered areas. Because quick wins at the outset will likely propel you to tackle harder spaces with more ease, I've tailored this checklist to start in sentimental-free areas before slowly increasing in difficulty. Complete just one checklist item per week; alternately, if you feel exceptionally motivated, cross out two or more in a single tidying session. And of course, if some items don't apply, move right on to the next one!

- ❑ 1. Personal care and beauty products
- ❑ 2. Bathroom shelves and drawers
- ❑ 3. Under bathroom sink
- ❑ 4. Bathtub and showers
- ❑ 5. Sheets, pillowcases, and blankets
- ❑ 6. Towels and washcloths
- ❑ 7. Medicine
- ❑ 8. First aid supplies
- ❑ 9. Cleaning supplies
- ❑ 10. Powder room storage area
- ❑ 11. Master bedroom nightstands
- ❑ 12. Under master bed
- ❑ 13. Master bedroom dresser drawers
- ❑ 14. Master bedroom closets
- ❑ 15. Kid room nightstands
- ❑ 16. Kid room dresser drawers
- ❑ 17. Kid room closets
- ❑ 18. Kid room under bed
- ❑ 19. Toys and stuffed animals

- ❑ 20. Guest room nightstand
- ❑ 21. Guest room dresser drawers
- ❑ 22. Guest room closet
- ❑ 23. Guest room under bed
- ❑ 24. Entryway/mudroom closet
- ❑ 25. Shoes and boots
- ❑ 26. Coats, jackets, and other seasonal gear
- ❑ 27. Pots, pans, and baking sheets
- ❑ 28. Utensils and silverware
- ❑ 29. Food storage containers
- ❑ 30. Everyday plates, cups, and mugs
- ❑ 31. Fancy china plates, cups, wine glasses
- ❑ 32. Miscellaneous kitchen drawers
- ❑ 33. Pantry, refrigerator, and freezer
- ❑ 34. Kitchen appliances
- ❑ 35. Kitchen surfaces
- ❑ 36. Platters and serving trays
- ❑ 37. Desk surface and drawers
- ❑ 38. Office paperwork

- ❏ 39. Mail and magazines
- ❏ 40. Craft supplies
- ❏ 41. School and office supplies
- ❏ 42. Books, movies, video games, and board games
- ❏ 43. Living room furniture, including coffee table and side tables
- ❏ 44. Outdoor toys
- ❏ 45. Tools and shed
- ❏ 46. Vehicle interior(s) and garage
- ❏ 47. Sports equipment
- ❏ 48. Exercise equipment
- ❏ 49. Junk drawer(s)
- ❏ 50. Party and holiday decor
- ❏ 51. Wrapping paper/gift bags
- ❏ 52. Attic/basement storage

The Five Pillars

Sustainable minimalists declutter with the planet in mind.

Marie Kondo's version of "spark joy" decluttering introduced millions to the "less is more" movement, and Kondo deserves applause for ushering the concept of tidiness into mainstream conversation. But Kondo and other prominent minimalists fall short by failing to advocate for *responsible* decluttering. And while they certainly encourage donation, they do not offer tangible advice on how or where, exactly, to let go of clutter in ways that minimally impact the planet.

While many minimalists declutter by throwing items in the trash, *sustainable* minimalists understand that seeking out, contacting, and schlepping unwanted possessions to appropriate donation sites can be both stressful and time consuming; still, they do it anyway. And while some

The end goal is not a tidy home; the end goal is a fundamental shift in one's relationship with possessions. possessions—especially ones that are broken or obsolete—will certainly be trashed, sustainable minimalists work tirelessly to send as little to the landfill as possible throughout the duration of the job.

Second, sustainable minimalists understand that decluttering is one step of a much larger journey. Without intention, this could result in an endless cycle of decluttering and purchasing behaviors. The end goal is not a tidy home; the end goal is a fundamental shift in one's relationship with possessions. Over time, this shift alters purchasing behavior, often quite drastically.

In every room, sustainable minimalists follow the five pillars of responsible decluttering:

1. Choose Quality over Quantity

2. Measure True Value

3. Ask the Tough Questions

4. Remove, but Don't Toss

5. Analyze What's Left

1. Choose Quality over Quantity

Be a curator, not a collector. Museum curators do not keep every piece of artwork or every ancient ceramic ever created. Instead, they display the best of the best within the museum's walls. As parents and homeowners, it is prudent to adopt a similar mindset. Trends will come and go, but a sustainable home will never go out of style. Your goal is not to keep the trendiest things, but to keep the best of a collection of similar items.

Be a curator, not a collector. If offered a choice, consider quality. Quality products are often made of solid wood and metal. Plastic often (but not always!) lends itself to cheaply-made items. Weak materials, like wicker or insect- and fungus-susceptible bamboo, may also not be durable enough to withstand the test of time.

When paring down your items, keep in mind the following quality-related considerations:

- Quality furniture is made of real wood, not particleboard. Aspire to keep solid wood furniture that has been treated with non-toxic dyes and water-based lacquers.

- Instead of keeping the comfiest or softest blanket, pillow, or bedding, read the items' labels and keep ones made with natural fibers that are free from flame-retardant chemicals and volatile organic compounds like formaldehyde.

- Does your child have five sets of blocks? Look at their collection through the lens of quality. Many parents shy away from plastic toys due to plastic's toxicity. Which blocks will last for future children? Which sets of blocks do not present a health danger?

- Do you have two spatulas, one silicone and one plastic? Consider placing the plastic spatula in the donation box. Keep the silicone spatula, as silicone boasts high heat-resistance and low toxicity.

- Remember that a broken, ripped, or stained item is no longer considered "quality." These possessions should either be repaired, if possible, or trashed.

2. Measure True Value

I have been fortunate to chat with many minimalists on my podcast over the past two years. In these interviews, I have heard a singular sentiment over and over again: in the throes of tidying, we tend to forget that true value is dependent on utility.

Every item has a fundamental purpose for existence. While a chair is meant to be sat on, a candle is meant to give light. Sustainable minimalists understand the difference between using an item in the present versus holding onto an item in the hopes of using it in the future. Possessions that are not regularly used have no real value, and when we store unused items for even *one day*, we prevent these items from reaching both their purpose and their potential.

Let's say you're storing a working microwave in your basement. You're not currently using the microwave; instead, it's collecting dust. Applying the concept of utility informs us that the microwave has no true value to you or anyone else because it isn't being used *right now* for its intended purpose (which is, of course, to warm food). But if you donated or sold that microwave to someone who could use it, you would immediately restore its value while also saving the recipient from having to purchase a brand new one.

Many consumers balk at the idea of donating or selling perfectly decent items, and that's understandable, as items cost money. But thanks to constant product turnover and innovation, electronics and appliances quickly become obsolete. Giving that microwave to someone in your community who needs it to warm food *right now* decreases the chances of finite resources, including fossil fuels, copper, other metals, and water, being extracted from the earth to make another microwave.

I often hear aspiring minimalists vocalize their desire to save items for their children once they are grown. But because most items tend to decrease in value over time, chances are your children won't want the items you've diligently saved. Take that microwave, for example. Will your child happily schlep that fifteen- or twenty-year-old microwave to their first apartment? Because goods are cheap—and because new microwaves can cost as little as fifty dollars—the answer is likely no.

Waiting five or ten years to donate an unused item will drastically reduce the item's chances of achieving its level of utility. This is particularly true in the cases of appliances and electronics. A flat-screen television in a storage unit could be given away and used in the present. But in a year or two, that flat-screen will be significantly less desirable to potential buyers because it will have been replaced by newer, shinier, sleeker models. Consider passing on or selling items in storage *right now*, while they're still considered up to date.

If you're having trouble parting with an item, ask yourself whether you could restore its value by giving it to someone who would *actually* use it. I registered for a trifle bowl just before my wedding nearly ten years ago, and although I had great intentions to make many trifles, I haven't made a single one. Probability informs me that if I haven't made a trifle in the last decade, chances are I'm not going to make one anytime soon. Donating the trifle bowl to someone who actually makes trifles will restore the item's utility, free up space in my kitchen, and prevent the receiver from purchasing one that's new. If I do have the sudden urge to make a trifle in the future, I can easily borrow a trifle bowl from a loved one.

3. Ask the Tough Questions

As you declutter, there may come a time (or many!) when you'll find yourself defeated. In these instances, ask yourself these curated questions to ease the difficulty associated with burdensome decluttering decisions:

Would You Keep It If You Downsized?

Although my family lives in the suburbs, my husband and I have big dreams to move to the city after our daughters grow into established adults. This one-day move from house to apartment will require us to significantly curtail our possessions. When faced with difficult decluttering questions in the present, I often find myself envisioning our future city apartment and wondering whether or not we would take a specific item or group of items when we do indeed move. This question tends to both anchor my efforts and provide clarity around which items are actually important.

Like gas, clutter expands to fill its container, and consumers tend to fill their spaces with possessions. Even if you have no plans to downsize, consider asking yourself the downsizing question when decluttering as a means of distinguishing what is essential from glorified clutter.

Would You Replace It If Broken?

When my mobile phone suddenly died, I cancelled everything on my schedule and replaced my phone within hours. But when my garlic press snapped? I made do and minced with a knife instead.

When an item breaks, we either rush to replace it, or we adapt. Use this logic when making difficult decluttering decisions: would you drop everything and immediately replace the item in question if it broke, or would you learn to live without it?

What's the Worst That Could Happen If You Let It Go?

Good books are my great loves, and I keep a small but curated collection of my favorites. When I found myself wanting to reread *The Catcher in the Rye*, I first searched my bookshelf. My earmarked copy wasn't there, and I was perplexed. I hunted high and low, even rummaged through places I knew it wouldn't be because I was certain I would never have donated such a beloved book. But after days of fruitless searching, I was forced to face an unfortunate reality: I must have donated it and forgotten.

While I was initially annoyed at myself for donating such a beloved possession (What was I *thinking*?), I simply ambled over to the library and checked out their copy.

Many people struggle with the fear that they may declutter an item and end up needing it later, and this fear scares them into overflowing their basements, garages, and attics with stuff. And while you may associate decluttering with a potential dire lack in the future, such doom-and-gloom notions are usually unfounded. If you let a possession go and find yourself needing it later, what's the worst that could happen? Would you be able to attain the item by borrowing, thrifting, or even buying it again? Unless the item in question is one-of-a-kind, the answer is usually yes.

Do You Feel Guilty?

Guilt is a powerful emotion, and it tends to hold us back from making important decluttering decisions. But your home is not a storage space for your past or a holding cell for others' possessions. It is a living space for your present life. The most guilt-inducing possessions, by far, are sentimental items, including trinkets from your childhood and mementos from deceased loved ones. And precisely because sentimental clutter is laden with both emotions and memories, such items often bring you down and hold you back. When your home is overwhelmed with remembrances of the past, it becomes difficult to make room for new memories.

Enable the singular to represent the whole. As you begin the difficult process of paring down items that once belonged to a loved one, consider instead how best to be intentional with the possessions you do decide to keep. Choose one item to represent a collection of items, such as a single teacup and saucer from your grandmother's china instead of the entire set, or one necklace your mother always wore instead of her entire costume jewelry collection. Keeping just that one teacup and saucer or just that one necklace, then, will enable the singular to represent the whole. You can also consider making a keepsake box to memorialize a deceased family member. Have a clear reason for saving each item in the keepsake box, because when you are clear about the items you definitely want to keep, it becomes easier to let go of the ones that aren't quite as special. Harness the power of your computer as you tidy: scan important paperwork, old photographs, childhood artwork, and more as a means of organizing clutter while retaining the sentiment.

Unneeded and unloved gifts are similarly guilt-inducing. But gift-givers are under no false notions that receivers will hold onto their gifts for perpetuity, and they don't intend to burden you with an item you feel guilted into keeping, either. For gift-givers, the *act* of giving is the gift–keeping gifts simply because they were given does no one any good. Think about the last present you gave someone. Would you prefer that they enjoy it and pass it along, or would you prefer that they hold onto it forever, despite the fact that your gift takes up space, causes emotional stress, and requires time and energy to maintain?

Many declutterers find themselves reluctant to let go of items simply because they were expensive. The sad truth is that items cost money, and once purchased, the transaction is complete and the money is gone. Realizing you spent hard-earned money on items you did not need or use can be an uncomfortable experience. As you declutter—and as you experience guilt over those overly expensive purchases—sit with your buyer's regret and learn to understand the root cause as a means of informing your future spending behavior.

4. Remove, but Don't Toss

Sustainable minimalists find homes for unwanted possessions whenever possible, *even though* responsible decluttering demands time, effort, and energy.

When I first started decluttering, I found myself utterly discouraged to realize that I had boxes filled with unwanted possessions but no one to give them to. Finding homes for my clutter beyond the landfill took more time than the decluttering did; it also required significant mental energy.

While it would certainly be simplest to toss unwanted items in the trash, sustainable minimalists find homes for unwanted possessions whenever possible, *even though* responsible decluttering demands time, effort, and energy. Many declutterers schedule specific time on their calendars for decluttering, because making one-hour appointments within the home discourages procrastination. Consider scheduling time on the back end, too, as doing so will enable you to discard, donate, and sell unwanted possessions in ways that do not harm the planet. If you plan to tackle the garage, let's say, and believe you can tidy the entire space in one weekend, block off the following weekend, too, so that you have the time you need to contact local charities, sell the items in good condition, and responsibly dispose of those you determined to be trash.

Should you sell or should you donate? I strongly advocate for selling high-demand, quality pieces whenever possible. The benefits to selling over donating are twofold. First, selling puts money in your pocket. Second, an exchange of funds for goods means the buyer will likely care for the item more than if they had acquired it for free.

From an environmental standpoint, it's best to keep your cast-off items in your community, as shipping fewer packages emits less carbon into the atmosphere. Consider churches, hospitals, schools, libraries, animal shelters, homeless shelters, women's shelters, halfway homes, food banks, senior centers, day cares, prisons, and charity shops before shipping an item to a national charity. To help you responsibly declutter, I have listed donation ideas for dozens of common household items in the appendix.

5. Analyze What's Left

After you've decluttered, your home may not feel as light, airy, and spacious as you'd hoped. Once the job is complete, zero in on these five oft-overlooked issues:

Too Much Furniture

When professional stagers prepare a home for sale, they first remove 80 percent of the homeowner's furniture. Next, they replace select pieces with smaller versions.

Home stagers understand that using fewer, smaller pieces makes homes feel bigger. If you find yourself constantly side-stepping end tables, floor lamps, and arm chairs, you may have too much furniture. Consider donating or selling the excess.

Refrigerator Woes

Refrigerator door clutter creates unnecessary visual overstimulation. Experiment with a clutter-free fridge for one week by removing absolutely every item from its face. Place your child's notable school papers in their baby book. Extract the important information from party invitations, too, then recycle the physical invitation. And photographs? Place them in a photo album.

Over the course of seven days, you may come to appreciate the blank space that a clutter-free refrigerator offers. If, however, it feels too bare for your liking, be intentional about which items you choose to display. Remember the cardinal rule of minimalism: less is always more.

Overstuffed Bookshelves

Cramped bookshelves beg to be organized. Combat book-related clutter by arranging books in ascending order. Push books to the front of shelves and line them up evenly to create a smooth face. To break up the visual monotony of book spine after book spine, intersperse a trinket here or there, or turn a few books horizontally.

Excessive Wall Art

Although many assume that bare walls demand artwork, excessive wall art detracts from the clean lines and visual simplicity many minimalists seek. Challenge the assumption that your walls *need* art: if the art serves no purpose other than filling empty space, remove a few wall hangings. If after one week you decide to rehang your artwork, do so because you have determined that the pieces genuinely *add* to your home's aesthetic, not detract from it.

Out-of-Control Collections

Back before I described myself as a sustainable minimalist (and back before I understood how unsustainable it is to travel frequently by air), my husband and I traveled often. I found myself in the habit of bringing home a teapot from each of the various countries we visited to memorialize each vacation. But as the number of trips we embarked on increased, I found myself in possession of more and more exotic teapots. I realized that, while my teapots were individually beautiful, they were an inconsistent, mismatched mess when displayed together.

When you exhibit too many of something, each item competes for attention. You never actually *see* any of the individual items in the collection, either; you tend to only view the collection as a whole. This problem can easily be solved by displaying less. Consider rotating the pieces in your collection every few months. Doing so will empower the items on display to rise to the forefront and garner the attention they deserve.

Responsible Kitchen Decluttering

The kitchen is the heart of the home, and for good reason: despite the frenetic quality of daily life, we gather with our families to break bread in this singular space each evening. But while the kitchen is the heart of the home, it also happens to be the hub. Because the kitchen is heavily trafficked, it also becomes the holding cell for dropped mail, unsigned school papers, car keys, and handbags.

A decluttered kitchen saves time, ensures cleanliness, and offers peace of mind. Although the average American kitchen holds a whopping 1,019 items, professional chefs argue that a fully functioning kitchen needs significantly less. as having more items does not necessarily correlate with better tasting food.[27]

Abide by Physical Boundaries

The kitchen, with its limited number of drawers and cabinets, responds well to decluttering that abides by physical boundaries. If you have more appliances than you can store in your kitchen, consider whether they are essential by musing over the concept of redundancy. Are you holding onto expendable appliances? Because bread can be baked in an oven, a bread maker can therefore be considered redundant. Panini presses and rice makers are also unnecessary, because you can utilize a skillet and saucepan, respectively, for both jobs.

Take care not to overstuff drawers and cabinets, as doing so will create additional headaches. Pay special attention to dishes, cups, and mugs: unless you have a large family, eight items per set tends to be enough.

As you put aside unwanted appliances and other houseware items for removal, know that, while working appliances should be sold or donated, broken appliances should not be placed in your curbside recycling bin. Curbside recycling programs are ill-equipped to handle such items and they will clog and break recycle machinery. Do not put small appliances in the trash either, as they leach toxic chemicals into groundwater when they break down in landfills. Instead, recycle broken appliances at designated electronic recycling events in your area.

Clear the Countertops

I keep very few items on my kitchen counters. I store knives in a drawer instead of in a knife block. I keep my blender in a cabinet, take it out each morning to make smoothies, and return it to the cabinet once I'm finished. I do not own a drying rack, either. I place wet dishes on a tea towel instead.

Clutter-free countertops are aesthetically pleasing, and the Clear Countertops Rule is a go-to minimalist trick in every room. For an instant refresh of your space, simply remove everything from the countertops.

Attack the Pantry

Place pantry staples in clear glass containers with well-fitting lids.

As you declutter and organize your pantry, rely less on expiration dates and more on your own intuition.

With the exception of baby formula, food product dates are not federally mandated, they are voluntarily included.[28] Further, expiration dates do not connote food safety, they connote peak food *freshness*. Because many manufacturers tend to be conservative with their product dating estimates, it is quite likely that you have plenty of food in your pantry, refrigerator, and freezer that is perfectly edible and safe.

If you do find yourself with food items that have gone stale or have otherwise turned, compost what you can, then wash and recycle packaging if possible. For plastic packaging, check the recycling triangle at the bottom to make sure your municipality accepts it before placing it in your recycling bin.

Items That Last Nearly Forever

White rice	Sugar
Dried beans	Cornstarch
Dried lentils	Vinegar
Honey	Dried pasta
Tea	Canned goods
Chocolate	Flour
Unsweetened cocoa	

Items That Last a Long Time (but Should be Checked)

Baking powder
Baking soda
Condiments
Oils
Dried egg pasta
Whole wheat pasta

While investing in commercial storage systems to organize your pantry may be tempting, storage "solutions" are often unnecessary. Instead of buying new bins, baskets, and containers, use mason jars to organize food items effortlessly. Be sure to label the jars and store them with the label facing outward. If you don't have mason jars on hand, simply repurpose jars from the supermarket by washing them thoroughly and removing their labels. If they have lingering smells, put two tablespoons of baking soda inside with a bit of water, shake, and leave it overnight. Any residual smells should be gone by morning. To remove particularly sticky labels from repurposed jars, soak them in lemon essential oil before peeling.

Real Life Sustainable Minimalists

How Many Is Too Many?

I used to be a wooden spoon junkie. I had wooden spoons of various shapes and sizes all over my kitchen and at the ready for any foods that needed stirring. But when I started my minimalism journey eight years ago, I took a hard look at those wooden spoons and asked myself a simple yet powerful question: How many do I *need*?

I'm not an octopus. I only have two arms with one hand attached to each. How many wooden spoons could I even use at once? The answer, of course, is two. So I simplified my wooden spoon collection to two and I have never looked back. (And yes, every sauce, soup, and batter is adequately stirred!)

Because I've drastically simplified the number of items in my kitchen, I can almost always find what I need when I need it.

If the vegetable peeler isn't in the drawer, I know it's in the dishwasher. And if the dishwasher happens to be running, the side of a spoon or a paring knife works just as well for peeling.

Because my drawers and cupboards are not jam-packed with stuff, my kitchen is more peaceful. Finding what I need to prepare meals is easier, and my kids—who have the honorable job of emptying the dishwasher—can easily put items back where they belong.

I maintain my decluttered kitchen by practicing daily routines. We clear and wipe the counters daily. We run the dishwasher every night and put the clean dishes away each morning. I also regularly check-in to see if each item in the kitchen still serves me. Have I used that Bundt pan or spiralizer in the last year? If not, I toss it in the donation box.

When I made the decision to simplify my kitchen, what I really did was make the decision to simplify my life. And that's a decision I benefit from every single day.

ROSE LOUNSBURY, episode #017 podcast guest
roselounsbury.com

Toy Tidiness

Wooden toys tend to be durable and non-toxic.

It is often the case that parents simply do not declutter their kids' toys enough. Despite their best efforts, their homes remain bursting at the seams. The solution is simple: conduct a second, ruthless toy declutter.

Toys to Responsibly Discard

- Noisy, light up toys
- Toys that do not encourage imaginative play
- Unloved stuffed animals
- Unused toys
- Damaged or broken toys

- Toys with missing pieces
- Toy collections that are rarely enjoyed
- Toys with screens
- Toys made from soft plastic

Toys to Consider Keeping

- Favorite stuffed animals
- Toys that enhance imaginative play (doctor kits, dress-up clothes)
- Toys that encourage gross motor skills (crawl tunnels)
- Toys that encourage fine motor skills (wooden peg puzzles, building blocks)
- Educational toys (puzzles, activity books)
- Family games

As you declutter your child's toys, choose quality by keeping ones made of wood, cotton, metal, and natural rubber; donate lower-quality toys made of plastic. For toys your child has outgrown, you can donate them or pass them along to younger friends in your community. Remember that smart decluttering is anchored in quality, not quantity, so spend significant time analyzing duplicates. How many sets of blocks does your child need? How many shape-sorting activities are indeed essential?

After you've determined which toys will stay, involve your child in the organizing process (if they're old enough to understand). Encourage them to command ownership of the space, as doing so increases the chances that toys will be in their correct spots. Have your child give a "tour" of their play space and show everyone where everything goes. This practice will reinforce their knowledge of where items belong.

If your home's designated space for toys is small, consider enacting more rigid toy boundaries. The Treasure Chest method gives each child a treasure chest to store their favorite toys. Your child can only keep what fits in their respective chest. If an item doesn't fit, urge them to reconsider favorites. Alternately, embrace toy rotation as a powerful means of curbing toy clutter. Repurpose seven to ten cardboard boxes and split all the household toys into them, making sure to place a variety of toys within each. Every few days, present just one box to your child. At the end of the day, clean-up is simple: all the toys go back into their box.

Decluttering Maintenance

Ensure your home stays tidy by performing daily maintenance.

The work is not complete after you've decluttered, and your home will not magically remain tidy without consistent, daily maintenance. Use the following strategies to ensure that your newly decluttered home stays that way for the long haul.

Be the Gatekeeper

Every possession demands time, effort, and energy to maintain, so empower yourself to step into the role of household gatekeeper. As gatekeeper, you decide which items you grant admittance into your home and check everything else at the door.

I am a ruthless gatekeeper. I politely decline the T-shirts my daughters receive for sports participation. I "forget" to take the party favors when leaving kids' birthday parties. We do not stop at the dentist office treasure chest. And when returning from the mailbox, I first head to the recycle bin in the garage to discard the junk mail. Be intentional about what you grant admittance into your home. Remember that unnecessary stuff creates clutter, and clutter takes more than it gives.

Incorporate Decluttering into Your Daily Routine

When decluttering becomes a habit, you naturally find yourself on the lookout for things you can responsibly unload as you move about your day. Make decluttering less of a big to-do and more of a quiet household chore that is best performed daily. As you wash dishes or fold clothes, keep an eye out for items you don't use or need. I keep a donation box in my garage and I slowly fill it with these kinds of items. When the box is full, I donate its contents.

Beware of Piles

Piles are delayed decisions. Instead of placing like items into neat piles and vowing to tackle them later, tackle them now. Consider the Five-Minute Rule as a means of gaining perspective. Can you reasonably clean up the pile in five minutes or less? If so, clean it up right away. Doing so will save time, lessen your mental load, and keep clutter at bay.

Enact Ten-Minute Cleanups

Like a street sweeper, I once followed my young daughters around the house, tidying every mess they created. I felt overburdened by the clutter and resentful that the cleaning always fell on my shoulders. On particularly long days at home, I found myself unable to keep up with their heightened levels of destruction. After putting Ani and Lara to bed, I would spend the next hour picking up the house even though I was utterly exhausted.

One evening, as I glanced at the dinner mess I hadn't yet tackled, my eyes drifted to the play room where dozens of toys littered the carpet. I decided I'd had enough. "Ten-minute cleanup!" I bellowed.

My husband and daughters didn't move. They had no idea what a ten-minute cleanup was. I wasn't completely sure, either, as I hadn't yet fully formulated the idea in my mind. But I refused to back down. I pointed in the direction of the toy room and instructed them to clean until the timer went off. I zeroed in on the kitchen while the girls tidied their toys with Haig's assistance. To my surprise, the major messes were mostly tidy when the timer went off ten short minutes later.

From that evening on, Ten-Minute Cleanup became a well-ingrained staple in my household. Instead of following your children around and cleaning their inevitable messes, consider enacting a more formal cleanup routine that harnesses help from every household member. Doing so will lessen your burden, improve your sanity, and teach your children to care for your shared space.

Make Donating a Family Affair

Children are generous by nature.[29] Help your child experience the joy that comes from giving by prioritizing donating as a family. At the end of each season, work with your child to gather clothes that are no longer worn and toys that are no longer played with. Encourage them to find a few items to contribute without your direction. Make decluttering a teachable moment by bringing your child to the donation center for drop-off. Doing so will help them recognize that their efforts are both needed and appreciated.

Common Concerns and How to Overcome Them

"I just don't have time to declutter my whole home."

I won't sugarcoat it: an entire home declutter takes months, if not a year or more. But if you dedicate just twenty minutes a day to decluttering, your efforts will likely snowball. Remember that whole-home decluttering is a marathon, not a sprint, and even sporadic good-faith efforts make a difference.

"My spouse and kids are reluctant to pare down their belongings. What do I do?"

Pushing family members into a lifestyle they aren't ready for will likely backfire. Instead, focus on your belongings, as well as all the other spaces in your home that will benefit from decluttering, including common rooms like the kitchen, living room, and bathrooms. Tidying the areas you have control over will enable you to experience the benefits of minimalism without fostering family discord.

"I've never been an organized person. What organization supplies do I need to make sure my efforts stick?"

An organized home is a natural result of owning fewer possessions. If you have fewer items, you will spend less time and energy trying to keep them organized. Focus less on buying the right baskets and bins (which comprise an entire industry in itself), and focus more on paring down. When it's time to organize, reuse items you already have instead of spending money on unnecessary organizational items. I use

An organized home is a natural result of owning fewer possessions.

a baby food jar to store my bobby pins, and I organize my daughters' underwear and socks within lidless shoeboxes in their drawers.

CHAPTER 3

Sustainable Minimalism on a Budget

Prominent sustainable minimalist influencers tend to portray simple living through rose-colored glasses. Eco-conscious social media feeds overflow with images of aesthetically-pleasing products, not upcycled or refurbished ones. As the popularity of reduction-based living continues to increase among consumers, such emphasis on newness perpetuates

Decluttering is a direct consequence of abundance, and making the *choice* to live minimally in itself demands a certain privilege. the notion that sustainable minimalism is an elitist lifestyle reserved only for those with disposable incomes. Decluttering is a direct consequence of abundance, and making the *choice* to live minimally in itself demands a certain privilege.

Admittedly, there is some truth to this reputation of exclusivity. While organic food is more eco-friendly than pesticide-laden produce, organic food is both more expensive and nonexistent in food deserts without access to healthier options. Food deserts are most often found in low-income, minority communities—wealthy, predominately white neighborhoods contain an average of four times as many supermarkets as predominantly black ones.[30]

Then there are the higher price tags on eco-friendly products. While many goods have green alternatives—and while the luxury of choice is indeed a major benefit for consumers—green products are almost always more expensive than their conventional counterparts. Hybrid cars, for example, boast fewer tailpipe emissions than conventional vehicles, yet they also cost an average of $4,650 more than their gas-guzzling counterparts.[31] Ethical and sustainable clothing also suffers from the price tag problem: while eco-conscious clothing brands implement fair wages and responsible manufacturing practices, the garments they sell are almost always significantly more expensive than fast fashion. Price is a major factor for shoppers, and hefty price tags on eco-friendly products further sustainable minimalism's reputation of inaccessibility.

Sustainability, Minimalism, and Frugality

Despite its elitist reputation, eco-friendly living isn't just for the privileged. In fact, the opposite is true: people who live in developing countries have significantly lower carbon footprints than those in developed ones.[32] And whereas consumption hurts the planet and fills our houses with stuff, being intentionally frugal is a powerful way to be eco-friendly.

Sustainable minimalists naturally tend to be intrinsically frugal, as they keep the bigger picture in mind.

Being frugal, though, is often associated with being cheap, and while public opinion tends to shun frugality as a result, spending less money complements a lifestyle rooted in reduction. Indeed, being frugal increases financial security, decreases stress and anxiety, contributes to a minimally-minded household, and prevents unnecessary items from one day filling your local landfill.

Sustainable minimalism on a budget isn't revolutionary; in fact, it's as simple as buying less, borrowing more, and prioritizing quality secondhand items. It's also about committing to becoming a conscious consumer who makes intentional purchasing decisions instead of mindless ones.

Are You a Conscious Consumer?

- A conscious consumer deliberately slows down the purchasing process and makes intentional purchasing decisions instead of buying mindlessly.

- A conscious consumer demands transparency from companies and is not afraid to pass on items unaligned with their values.

- A conscious consumer distinguishes wants from needs and refuses to be swayed by marketing gimmicks.

- A conscious consumer understands their purchasing power, and aspires to improve the world with their dollars.

Seven Habits of Conscious Consumers

1. Build in Buffer Zones

When I signed Ani up for spring T-ball, I knew she would need a glove. I didn't want to buy one, especially if it turned out that Ani disliked T-Ball. But I forgot to ask my friends if they had a right-handed glove I could borrow; the task simply slipped my mind. One week later, I found myself down to the wire with just two days until practice and no T-ball glove. I had no choice but to purchase a glove online, complete with expedited shipping.

Ani *did* end up disliking T-Ball, and she had no use for that glove after the six-week session concluded. If I had attempted to borrow one the second after I signed her up, I could have acquired it by other means and thus saved twenty dollars. Instead, I waited until the last minute. And in those last minutes, I had no choice but to buy new.

When you're down to the wire, you tend to abandon any and all attempts at intentional purchasing. If you know you need an item, give yourself the necessary time to acquire it by alternate means. Can you borrow one from a friend, or buy one secondhand? By giving yourself a healthy buffer zone, you empower yourself to decide when or if you buy, but only after you exhaust all other options.

2. Enact Monthly Budgets

There is absolutely nothing glamorous about writing out—and sticking to!—a monthly budget. Discussing your budget at the start of every month can be awkward, as conversations about money often are. Yet these conversations are necessary, because a budget makes spending habits clear, for better or for worse. Convening at the start of every month to tweak the budget ensures that you and your partner are on the same page. The practice encourages you to analyze the previous month's spending, and forces you to sit with a wildly uncomfortable feeling if you overspent.

Enacting a monthly budget is complemented by having a family vision. When you and the other members of your family are vocal about what the family unit deems important, it becomes easier to steer the monthly budget toward your values.

3. Flex Your Purchasing Power

Spending hard-earned money on products and services from ethical and eco-conscious corporations sends the message to the market that you desire to see sustainable options. Yet finding ethical, sustainable, and non-toxic products amidst all the environmentally damaging ones can be both a difficult and time-consuming task. Consider frequenting two websites to inform your purchasing decisions before buying a single thing:

EWG.org: The Environmental Working Group (EWG) is a nonprofit, non-partisan organization dedicated to helping consumers live healthier lives on a healthy planet. The site encourages users to make smart purchasing decisions by comparing similar products' toxicity and environmental impact. I particularly appreciate EWG's Skin Deep Guide to Cosmetics, which rates 70,000 personal care products.

Buymeonce.com: Instead of buying a cheap product over and over, Buy Me Once believes that buying a single, quality product with a comprehensive warrantee is the smartest, most eco-friendly choice. The site independently researches various items and highlights brands with the best guarantees and the most responsible manufacturing processes. I often use the site's search feature before making an expensive purchase, then I either purchase directly through the website or from a retailer of my choice.

Avoid Greenwashed Products

Sadly, because there are consumers who demand environmentally-friendly products, corporations tout misleading claims to sound more eco-conscious than they actually are. It's called greenwashing, and even the most conscious of consumers find themselves duped by innuendos, imagery, and outright lies.

Greenwashing Facts

Greenwashing is a marketing ploy that promotes the perception that an organization is environmentally friendly.

Greenwashing occurs when a company spends more time and money claiming to be green than actually implementing business and manufacturing practices that minimize their environmental impact.

The prevalence of greenwashing is growing. As consumers increasingly demand eco-friendly products, marketers use greenwashing as a means to sell more products to customers who identify as green-leaning.

Greenwashing is about profit. Corporations desire to sell products. If they can sell by claiming to be green, they will.

Greenwashing can be quite explicit, and once uncovered, it's easy to identify. The most blatant example of greenwashing in recent history is the 2015 Volkswagen scandal, when eleven million diesel-burning cars worldwide were fitted with defeat devices—motor vehicle software that could detect when they were being tested and change emission performances accordingly. Such greenwashing was both explicit and illegal.

But greenwashing is more often implicit. Spot greenwashing by first inspecting a product's packaging with a fine-toothed comb. If its imagery or wording suggests a reality that is too good to be true, it probably is. And if a product boasts complicated verbiage that only a scientist could decipher, that, too, is likely greenwashing. If there is no supporting information to explain *how* a product adheres to its claims, it's likely smoke and mirrors. Companies that have woven sustainability into their mission—not just into their marketing— will have detailed information about their efforts on their websites.

Support Local Businesses

Buying locally is a powerful way to strengthen community resilience.

When you buy local, your money stays local. Instead of heading to a big-name chain, consider purchasing items within your community. The practice supports your neighbors, encourages job creation, curbs carbon emissions associated with product shipment over long distances, and in the case of food, reduces packaging waste.[33] Perhaps the biggest benefit to supporting your local economy is that it strengthens community resilience, a necessity for combatting future challenges associated with climate change.

4. Trust Reputable Certifications

Forget "all-natural," "fat-free," and other blanket marketing statements. Trusted, third-party certifications give consumers confidence that a product has met strict guidelines for health, environmental, or social concerns.

A common criticism of the certification process is that, because it often costs money for products to become certified, big corporations can pay third-party certifiers hefty up-front sums and smaller, mom-and-pop entrepreneurs are left out in the cold. Are certifications yet another marketing ploy?

Yes and no. Buy locally whenever possible, and reach out to the makers and growers in your community. Ask your local farmer if they follow organic growing practices. Similarly, inquire as to whether your local soap maker will provide a list of ingredients with their product. You may find that local product options meet third-party guidelines but are simply not adorned with universal emblems.

Labels, Explained

Although certifications are meant to impart confidence, many consumers find it difficult to discern what each different logo stands for. Below are some of the most common certifications, explained:

Certified B Corporation

Certified B Corporations are devoted to using business as a force for good, even at the expense of profit. The Certified B Corporation logo makes a strong statement about a company's social and environmental practices.

Fair Trade

Fair Trade certification ensures that craftsmen and women, farmers, fisherman, and more are paid living wages that fulfill basic household needs. The certification prohibits the use of the most harmful chemicals, too, and seeks to protect natural resources.

Forest Stewardship Council (FSC)

The FSC takes a stand against deforestation and certifies products derived from trees that are harvested from responsibly-managed and environmentally-conscious forests.

Global Organic Textile Standard (GOTS)

GOTS certifies textile products, like clothing, bedding, and more, that contain at least 95-percent certified organic fibers.

MADE SAFE®

MADE SAFE® identifies personal care and home products without toxic chemicals like endocrine disruptors, carcinogens, and high-risk pesticides.

USDA Certified Organic

A USDA Certified Organic label ensures that the food item contains 95 percent or more certified organic ingredients and is free of synthetic additives.

---

5. Assess Hidden Costs

Many minimalists understand that the cost of an item runs much deeper than its sticker price, and that's because every possession burdens buyers in the long-term with the two hidden costs of time and environmental impact.

Time

Items cost money, and you make money by working. Think less about a potential purchase in terms of its price tag—forget about the great "deal," too—and instead mull over how many hours of your life you'd have to work in order to make the purchase.

Here's an example. Facebook's all-knowing algorithm curates the ads users see, and as such, I often spy eco-friendly products embedded within my news feed. And because I occasionally engage with ads for clothes and shoes, countless ads from sustainable clothing companies intermingle with friends' status updates. Recently, Facebook placed an ad for chestnut ankle boots on my news feed. They weren't just any humdrum ankle boots—the company boasted attributes I value, including the fact that they give 10 percent of profits to environmental causes. And the boots? Quality shoemakers sewed them from natural materials by hand.

I really appreciated the look of these boots. I didn't just want them—I convinced myself I needed them. But with a hefty price tag of $224, they were expensive footwear. I did the math: assuming I earn $15 per hour, I would have to work 14.9 hours to pay for those boots. When I reframe this purchase and others in terms of hours off my life, unnecessary items often lose their appeal.

You can buy more time by buying less stuff. It is also prudent to calculate lost time by considering how much free time the potential purchase will require in the future. How often will you care for the item to keep it pristine? How upset will you be when the item inevitably loses its newness? Are there other things you would prefer to do with your free time than care for the possession?

While your time on this earth is finite, you can buy more time by buying less stuff.

Environmental Impact

The premise behind the market economy is fundamentally flawed. While capitalism promotes infinite consumption, our planet does not offer infinite resources. Nonrenewable

While capitalism promotes infinite consumption, our planet does not offer infinite resources. resources like water, oil, natural gas, and coal are often required for manufacturing; once used up, these limited resources cannot be replaced.[34] This is particularly concerning in the case of fossil fuels, as humanity is heavily dependent on them to supply the majority of our energy needs.

Packaging materials for shipments also have oversized environmental impacts. Plastic bags, plastic fillers, and polystyrene, also known as Styrofoam, are major contributors to micro-plastic pollution (discussed further in chapter 7). There are climate considerations associated with shipments, too: moving goods around the globe on trucks and planes generates unnecessary carbon emissions that warm our already warm planet.[35] Expedited shipping only increases emissions, as two-day shipping often requires air travel.[36] A powerful way to help the planet is to simply buy less.

Small Acts, Big Impacts

Want to be eco-friendly without spending money? Here are ten quick tips:

1. Snag Bottle Refunds

Bottle refund programs reduce litter and ensure return of highly desirable recyclables like glass and aluminum. Collect those cans and bottles and get a 5-cent refund if you live in one of eleven participating states: California, Connecticut,

Delaware, Hawaii, Iowa, Maine, Massachusetts, Michigan, New York, Oregon, and Vermont.

2. Clean that Lint Trap

A clean filter in your dryer reduces drying time, which wastes less electricity.

3. Refuse (Unneeded) Free Stuff

Free pens. Free tee-shirts. Ketchup packets. If you don't need it, don't take it. Instead, save such items for others who actually do need them.

4. Surf Green

Ecosia.com plants trees with its ad revenue, so use it instead of Google when surfing the web. Simply make Ecosia your home screen, or download the browser extension to browse the eco-friendly way. Browse often on your phone? Download their free app for when you're on-the-go.

5. Turn Off Lights

There's no sense in lighting rooms you aren't using. You can save a bit of money by turning off lights. Know that switching out your incandescent bulbs for LEDs will save money in the long run, too.

6. Dry with Intention

When drying hands with paper towels in a public restroom, shake excess water off first, then dry the remainder with a single paper towel. Apply this logic to paper napkins, too:

instead of grabbing a whole stack at a restaurant, take just one or two.

7. Put Vampire Energy Suckers on Notice

GoogleTV and AppleTV set boxes, computers, modems, and DVD players suck significant energy when they are "sleeping." Unplug them when they're not in use and watch your electricity bill drop.

8. Carpool with Pride

Ridesharing decreases the amount of cars on the road, eliminates unnecessary carbon dioxide from entering the atmosphere, and saves money. (It saves you the hassle of driving, too!) Coworkers don't live nearby? No problem. Consider using one of countless rideshare apps to crowdsource your commute.

9. Turn Down the Water Heater

Most of us rarely—if ever—need tap water at its hottest, so why not turn down the water heater? It's as easy as turning a knob. The standard temperature for most water heaters is 140 degrees Fahrenheit. Try adjusting it to 130, or even 120 degrees, and see if you notice a difference. (You likely won't.)

10. Light Fires the Old-Fashioned Way

Stop buying plastic lighters and go back to matches instead. Back when smoking was popular, matches were given away everywhere for free. Now they're a little harder to find, but keep your eyes open at convenience stores and gas stations.

6. Sleep on It

Because e-commerce lowers barriers to buying, it has never been easier to make regrettable purchasing decisions. But everything is clearer in the morning. Get in the habit of saving items in your online shopping cart to giving yourself twenty-four hours to mull over the potential purchase. Use this self-created breathing room to ask yourself three critical questions, including:

Can You Get by without It a Bit Longer?

Said another way, is this purchase a need, or is it a want?

Consider the concept of utility: every item has a fundamental *purpose*. A sweater's purpose is not to be fashionable, it's meant to keep its wearer warm. Do you have other clothes that keep you sufficiently warm? Will the sweater you're eyeing perform its utility better than the other clothing items you already own? If so, how?

What Are the Alternatives?

On the occasions that you decide the item you're considering is a legitimate need, determine whether you can acquire the item by alternative means.

Take that sweater, for example. If you do decide you need a sweater for warmth, ask yourself whether you need that *specific* sweater. Can you purchase a different sweater through a secondhand vendor? Could you borrow a sweater from a family member until the weather warms?

Does the Item Speak to My Authentic Self?

Remember that consumers are aspirational spenders who often buy items that their *fantasy* selves would wear and use. Is the item you're spying an aspirational purchase that you hope will make you look smarter, more attractive, more eco-conscious, or something else? If the answer is yes, consider your affirmative a red flag.

Real Life Sustainable Minimalists

The Work-Spend Hamster Wheel

I'm a businesswoman, wife, and mother of three. I work hard both in and out of the home, and I value the work I do. It took me a long time to realize that I tied my work to my self-worth. Because working hard is what smart, successful people do, shopping, then, was my reward.

When my kids were bored, I bought a new toy to entertain them. And when *I* was bored, I scrolled through the websites of my favorite stores for clothes and trinkets to cure my unease. I can't pinpoint my exact moment of clarity, but when it occurred, I came to an overwhelming realization: I was stuck in a cycle of working hard, buying stuff to fulfill my inner disquiet, then working harder to pay for all the stuff I bought.

I'm still a work in progress and I continue to struggle with *not* buying in a culture that glorifies buying. But I do believe that the more you and I talk openly about conscious consumerism, the more mainstream the lifestyle becomes.

DEANNA M., podcast listener

7. Shift Your Spending Mindset

Consumers have been conditioned to seek out items with the lowest price tags. And while great sales are enticing, succumbing to deals may go against your best interests.

The paradox is this: despite our collective societal wealth, Americans tend to buy cheap stuff. Poor purchasing decisions are evident in cheap furniture that buckles and breaks, and in synthetic clothes that fade and pill after just a handful of washes. Through purchases, consumers have created a single-use society in which everything—from napkins, to diapers, to furniture, to clothing—is considered disposable.

Becoming a conscious consumer requires a countercultural and revolutionary mindset shift that seizes power from corporations and places it squarely in your, the consumer's, hands. Turn away from the cheap goods if you are financially able, and stop chasing sales, too. Rethink the perceived glamour associated with inexpensive items by considering the following mindset tweaks:

Know That the Cheapest Price Is Not the Fairest Price

When you seek out the cheapest price, you do so despite legitimate ethical and sustainable concerns. First, there are human ethics at play. Workers who made the item may not have been paid fair living wages; they likely toiled in unhealthy conditions, too.[37] Then there are numerous environmental issues: toxic waste disposal, water pollution, excessive carbon emissions, and more are corners that corporations may cut to bring you the cheapest possible price.

Consider Cost-Per-Wear (CPW)

While cheap price tags often result in disposable purchases, hefty ones scare consumers away. Adopting the cost-per-wear (CPW) strategy, however, is a realistic means of mitigating the price tag shock associated with ethical, eco-friendly, and well-made products.

CPW reframes purchases by quantifying value over time, and is calculated by adding an item's purchase price, then dividing that number by the total number of uses. Say you purchase a 100-percent wool sweater at $100 and wear it just one time. That wear cost you $100. But if you wear that sweater ten times, the CPW drops to $10. And because wool is an all-natural fiber, chances are you *will* wear that sweater closer to one hundred times, which would then drop the CPW to just $1. This sweater will also excel at performing its utility, because wool is an exemplary natural insulator.

Compare this wool sweater to a fast-fashion sweater bought on sale for $25. You might manage to wear it just five times (a CPW of $5) before the fabric pills and the garment loses its shape. Its synthetic fibers won't keep you particularly warm, either, so you won't wear it during the coldest winter days. Even though the $25 sweater was four times cheaper than the wool one, reframing the purchase this way makes the cheap sweater less appealing because the wool one—with its quality materials that withstand the test of time—has a significantly lower CPW.

Common Concerns and How to Overcome Them

"I'm not sure I have the time or energy to seek items out by alternative means. Amazon makes buying so easy."

Here's a secret: the internet makes borrowing and thrifting just as easy as buying off Amazon. Borrowing, repurposing, and upcycling are common ways in which sustainable minimalists acquire needed items without buying new, and because the savings and benefits are huge, doing so will likely motivate you to decrease your reliance on Amazon over time. We will discuss the ins and outs of online thrifting in chapter 9.

"Doesn't borrowing increase stress? I will have to give the item back one day. What if I ruin it or misplace it? Just thinking about it makes my anxiety skyrocket."

When you borrow, you *do* have to eventually return the item to its original owner. But buying is not an anxiety-free practice. When you buy, you are stuck with an item for life. Purchasing requires you to organize, maintain, clean, and store the item long after you are done needing it. There are stresses associated with *both* buying and borrowing, but borrowing saves money and does not harm the planet.

"I'm just not financially able to buy the most expensive items on the market."

Many consumers do not have the financial means to purchase the highest-quality items on the market simply because such items are often saddled with the heftiest price tags. A practical solution to this problem is to embrace quality secondhand, as thrift stores and online secondhand marketplaces tend to overflow with high-quality, working items at a fraction of the cost of their new counterparts. Seeking out hand-me-downs is a second way to acquire quality goods without spending money unnecessarily.

CHAPTER 4

Day-to-Day Minimalism with Kids

We owe it to our children to think critically about consumer culture. Overconsumption of both material goods and environmental resources impacts the health of the planet they stand to inherit.

Have children? If so, you've likely experienced the reality that kids–particularly, small kids–tend to require a lot of stuff and create a lot of waste. While parenting may present additional challenges to a lifestyle rooted in the tenets of sustainable minimalism, we owe it to our children to think critically about consumer culture. Overconsumption of both material goods and environmental resources impacts the health of the planet they stand to inherit.

Sustainable minimalists tend to parent differently. Because they prioritize experiences over possessions, their children often have fewer toys and participate in fewer extracurricular activities. They revere the concept of slow living as a means of prioritizing quality time together. Households rooted in simplicity are also quite concerned with passing eco-conscious ideals along to their children.

Parenting is hard work, and parenting the countercultural way is even harder. This chapter offers eight strategies to make it easier.

It Takes a Village

How do you practice eco-friendly, minimalist parenting? Spread the love by sharing your best tips on social media using the hashtag #sustainableminimalists.

Enact a Family Vision

You only have eighteen years with your children. Just eighteen summers, and eighteen birthdays. I have heard parents say time and time again, "Where does the time go?" and, "It seems like my child was born yesterday." Such statements convey lost time and missed opportunities.

While entrepreneurs spend significant time crafting vision statements and listing core values for their businesses, parents find themselves too caught up in the minutiae of parenthood to visualize the big picture. As a parent, you have the unique opportunity to be the CEO of your household. Instead of lamenting over lost time and fleeting childhoods, take small-scale, daily steps toward achieving an intentional family life.

It is absolutely possible to be intentional with your family's values and goals, and it starts by asking the question, "If we could be the best family we could be, what kinds of things would we be doing and saying?" Consciousness means having frank and frequent conversations with your partner about what matters versus what doesn't; it continues by choosing the big-picture vision you agreed upon every single day.

A parenting mantra complements your family vision by bringing the big picture to the forefront during instances of family discord. Ani is in elementary school now, and she has begun to ask difficult questions, like why her friends have technological devices that she doesn't. She also asks why we rarely go out to eat. My response to these questions and others like them is simple: "In this family, we do things differently." This is my parenting mantra, and I resort to it when Ani contrasts our family's values to what she observes in her friends'. The mantra has proven to be simple but effective, especially when I immediately follow it with gentle reminders about the wonderful things our family does differently.

Invest in Experiences

Research consistently finds that experiences confer lasting benefits to children, and that family vacations are an investment in your child's development.[38] Experiences exercise two systems in the limbic area of your child's brain: the Play system and the Seeking system.[39] And while the Play and Seeking systems tend to remain unexercised at home, children rely on the skills these systems provide during novel experiences. In turn, these experiences improve cognitive functioning, problem-solving, emotional expression, memory, language, and judgment.

Vacations are "happiness anchors," too. When families are faced with challenging times, reflecting on fond memories offers the perspective needed to approach problems with renewed vigor.[40] If yearly vacations aren't feasible for your family, know that investing in experiences does not have to break the bank. Quality time is a natural consequence of making intentional, daily choices to explore as a family. A hike, a visit to the nearby children's museum, or making the most of a staycation are powerful ways to invest in experiences without hefty upfront costs.

Schedule Slow Time

Scheduling downtime encourages your children to rest, relax, regroup, and recharge.

Birthday parties, sports practices, play dates, and more: if we let them, commitments will fill family schedules, and fast.

Haig and I signed Ani up for extracurriculars with gusto shortly after she turned five. She had swim lessons on Tuesdays, dance on Wednesdays, and our weekends were anchored by T-ball on Saturday mornings and soccer on Sunday afternoons. Haig and I desired to give Ani every opportunity within our means, and we assumed that saying yes to a multitude of novel experiences meant we were parenting well.

But not long after, I had a moment of clarity. I looked into the future and saw what our weekends would look like if we did not make changes: Haig would schlep one daughter to her extracurriculars, while I carted the other off to hers. Perhaps our paths would cross at home for dinner, perhaps not. And while I certainly desired to give my children every opportunity possible, the entire family would be swept away by obligations if we did not make changes, and soon.

The tenets of minimalism apply not just to clutter; they lend themselves to simplifying schedules, too. Research abounds on the benefits of extracurriculars. Children who participate in extracurriculars tend to do better academically than children who spend their free time using electronics and avoiding social situations; they also report higher levels of self-esteem.[41] [42] And while extracurricular activities are certainly important, too much of a good thing exists. An always on-the-go attitude often comes at the expense of the family, and resulting strain can create more harm than good. Children need parents to schedule slow time into the family calendar, as unscheduled time is key to character development and emotional health.[43]

These days, it is our family rule that each daughter may do up to two activities at a time. Although it can be difficult to decline invitations and sit some sports seasons out, I remind myself that the tenets of minimalism apply not just to clutter; they lend themselves to simplifying schedules, too.

Establish Gifting Strategies

My grandmother—God bless her soul—was an over-gifter. She showed her love by giving presents, and she showered my daughters with stuffed animals and coloring books every time we visited. She believed, as many do, that a holiday or a birthday is only a legitimate celebration if there are heaps of physical gifts. Curbing this long-held, societal belief can be difficult (especially for more ardent gift-givers), but it is possible.

Birthdays and holidays provide annual opportunities for over-gifting. As a result, they are constant threats to a sustainable minimalist's household. But low-gift and gift-free celebrations keep overconsumption in check, curb unnecessary clutter, and prevent high-pressure situations where children are forced to open gifts in front of a crowd. Abiding by a gifting strategy and communicating it clearly will reduce unnecessary presents.

Birthdays and Gifts

My daughters receive some presents from Haig and me on their birthdays, as well as from grandparents, aunts, and uncles. But we celebrate gift-free with their friends and extended family members. I request no presents on the party invitation in simple, plain language: "My daughter has everything she needs. Please, no gifts!"

Still, no one likes to attend a party empty-handed, so I ask on the invitation that each guest bring a wrapped children's book instead. As guests enter, I quietly put the wrapped books aside and don't mention them again until the party concludes. The books double as party favors: before guests leave, each child gets to choose a wrapped book to take home instead of a goody bag.

No-Present Birthdays are a Thing

There are plenty of ways to make your child feel special on their birthday without relying on gifts, such as:

- Ask for a handwritten note for your child to read when they're an adult. Reserve a binder for all the notes and collect them over the years. Even better, create a secret email address for your child and ask guests to write them an email on every birthday until they turn 18.

- Ask guests to bring a previously loved item that still has a lot of life left, like an outgrown toy or a handmade sweater with a story.

- Ask for donations to a charity of your or your child's choosing. If you send invitations, place the charity's direct link on the electronic invitation with detailed instructions.

- Ask guests to contribute to the party theme. If party-goers will be decorating cupcakes, ask invitees to bring the frosting and sprinkles. Building birdhouses? Ask guests to supply the glue and paint.

- Ask for monetary contributions. Encourage loved ones to contribute to your child's existing college fund and offer detailed instructions on how to do so. Alternately, ask family and friends to contribute toward a larger, more expensive gift. There are many websites designed to both begin this (sometimes awkward) conversation and streamline the process: **Plumfund.com** works well for younger children. **Goalsetter.co** is ideal for older children because the website includes the child in the savings process and encourages them to set savings goals.

If you attempt a no-gifts birthday, know that some guests will flat-out ignore your request and bring presents anyway. Remove emphasis from the presents and encourage your child to enjoy time with their closest friends and family members by putting the gifts aside until after the party concludes.

Navigating the Holidays

If you have ever bought more holiday gifts for your child than they needed, you're not alone. The market economy wants us to believe that love lies in *things* and that sentiment is directly proportional to price tags. A powerful way to combat a natural desire to over-gift is to be intentional about the holidays before buying a single item. A minimalist approach to gift-giving sets categorical limits so that each present satisfies a specific category, including the following:

- **Want:** A gift that attempts to satisfy the child's greatest want

- **Wear:** A wearable gift, including clothes, hats, winter gear, and more

- **Need:** A gift that satisfies a real need

- **Share:** A gift for everyone to enjoy, such as a gigantic set of Legos or a new swing set

- **Read:** A book or magazine

- **Experience:** A gift the entire family can experience together, such as tickets to a show, museum, or amusement park

Following a gifting framework takes the stress out of holiday shopping by allowing one to save money and decrease clutter. Consider discussing with your partner how to best be intentional with holiday gift-giving, then stick to what you determined to be appropriate.

It used to be that Haig and I would buy and buy around the holidays; after, we would stare in horror at the credit card bill. But these days, we follow the above framework quite rigidly. Before Christmas comes around, I create a shareable electronic document that lists the above gifting categories. Then we work together to determine the best gifts for each category and for each daughter. Once we have obtained a comprehensive list that we both agree on, we buy only the items on the list.

Real Life Sustainable Minimalists

Grace and Boldness

As I attempt to balance motherhood, minimalism, and low-waste living, I have learned that grace and boldness are vital.

First, grace. When I was a new mother, I was tired and busy all the time. Low-waste living required pre-planning and sacrifice, but some days I didn't have the bandwidth to do anything more than survive. Sustainability fell to the background, and I was ridiculously wasteful as a result. Giving myself grace instead of piling on the guilt kept me from completely throwing in the towel on my eco-conscious ideals.

Second, boldness. As my son grows, I find myself more willing and able to tackle sustainability in and out of the home. Some of my more extreme eco-friendly actions (No plastic! Only hand-me-downs!) have resulted in many side-eyes from friends and fellow mothers. It takes a special kind of person to go against the norm and parent differently, and I'm happy to be that person. I don't think I'm weird, but if I am, I'm fine with it. My kids are watching and learning, and so are other parents. I feel good knowing that my unconventional lifestyle sets the stage for real change.

LEE ANN K., podcast listener

Establish Toy Boundaries

When Ani was a toddler, she had an abundance of toys. Because children learn through play and children play with toys, I believed dozens of toys would provide her with diverse play experiences. But I observed noticeable differences in play *quality*. While dress-up clothes encouraged imaginative play and blocks developed fine motor skills, other toys—like her electronic camera with built-in games—resulted in the mindless pushing of buttons over and over again.

When it comes to toys, research finds that less is more. Children, especially toddlers, are more imaginative and focused when surrounded by *fewer* toys.[44] And while toys are certainly important for development, research also finds that basic toys are better.[45] Wooden blocks, vehicles, construction toys, and play food and utensils encourage quality play from boys and girls alike.

Then there's the plastic problem. Plastic toys tend to be inexpensive, and as such, they account for 90 percent of the toy market. But plastic toys are notoriously difficult—if not downright impossible—to recycle. And because plastic toys rarely withstand the test of time, they are discarded quicker than higher-quality items.[46]

There are potential health implications associated with plastic toys, too. As reported in a study on fertility, "Phthalates are often used to soften plastic toys and have been linked to birth defects, cancer, and diabetes."[47] [48] Because young children often put toys in their mouths, they are at an increased risk for health issues from plastic toys. As a general rule, it is prudent to stay away from flexible and soft plastic toys that are labeled #3 Polyvinyl Chloride (PVC). Be cautious of #7 Other, as Bisphenol A (BPA) leaches from these plastics and acts as a hormone disruptor.[49]

Although overindulgence may seem as though it's the new normal—and although overbuying for children always comes from a good place–giving too much and too often leads to a host of interpersonal difficulties that stem from an oversized sense of entitlement.[50] When you give your child the space to dream about earning and owning a very special possession, you also encourage them to aspire and learn coping skills.[51]

---

10 Questions to Ask Before Buying for Your Child

1. Does my child need this?

2. Did my child do something special to earn this?

3. What is the item made of?

4. Does the item spark curiosity and creativity?

5. Is this an item my child should save for and buy themselves?

6. Can the item be played with in more than one way?

7. Does our home have a place to put this item?

8. Will my child appreciate it?

9. Is the item developmentally appropriate?

10. Would this item be better given at a birthday or
    major holiday?

Commit to Quality Secondhand

For Christmas last year, Ani asked for a Barbie Dream House,
and I bristled. I consider Barbie Dream Houses and other
plastic toys that promote gendered or violent themes to be
junk culture, and I certainly didn't want to spend hard-earned
money buying into it. But I didn't want to crush Ani's Christmas
dreams or be a killjoy.

Low-waste parenting is about buying or otherwise acquiring quality items secondhand instead of buying new items that are junk.

My solution to the Barbie Dream House
conundrum was to ask around in my
community. Was anyone willing to part
with a Dream House? It just so happened
that a neighbor just down the street had
one her daughter no longer played with
and was happy to pass it along. In the end,
everyone won: my neighbor unloaded an
oversized possession, Ani received a
new-to-her Barbie Dream House on
Christmas morning, and I satisfied my
eco-minimalist values by preventing additional plastic from
entering the waste stream.

First-time parents often understandably shun pre-used gear,
toys, and clothes. Parents want the best for their children,
and many assume *best* is what's new, clean, and shiny. But

many parents wise up once their second child comes along, and that's because they have learned that the amount of time a child will realistically use an item is short. Low-waste parenting is about buying or otherwise acquiring quality items secondhand instead of buying new items that are junk. By committing to secondhand, you extend the lives of perfectly good toys, clothes, and gear while also saving a significant amount of money.

When buying secondhand, the secret lies in seeking out *quality* items that will withstand the test of time. When I was pregnant with Lara, I knew we would soon need a double stroller. I knew the brand I wanted; I knew, too, that its sticker price was a whopping $729. Yet the amount of time we would need a double stroller was short, as Ani would soon prefer to walk on her own. While we considered purchasing a new but cheaper stroller, we opted instead to purchase my desired stroller secondhand for a fifth of the cost of a new model. While the one we purchased was six years old and certainly not pristine, it wheeled. And a few short years later when we were ready to pass the double stroller on, I sold it for the *exact* price I had originally paid. Because we invested in quality secondhand, the stroller continued to have life well after my family outgrew it.

Secondhand baby and toddler clothing is a godsend. Because babies and toddlers grow fast, many clothing items found in thrift stores have been worn five times or less. Savvy secondhand shoppers can also find great deals on durable toys and books. Whenever you score a secondhand item, inspect it for both safety and cleanliness. Throw items made from fabric in the washing machine, and sanitize plastic and wood items in the kitchen sink.

In the instance of baby safety, however, newer is better for items that they sit, lie, or put much of their weight on. The American Academy of Pediatrics recommends that parents buy new car seats, and that cribs considered be manufactured after 2011. If you choose to obtain these items secondhand, do so from people you trust so you know how old the products are. And whenever you acquire secondhand gear, Google its manufacturer name and date to determine whether it has been recalled. We will discuss the ins and outs of twenty-first century thrifting—including how exactly to thrift—in chapter 9.

Keep the cycle of giving going by paying it forward: pass on your outgrown items to worthy recipients when the time comes. Remember that when you give away or sell no-longer-needed items, you halt new items from one day becoming waste. If your child's no-longer-used items hold significant emotional baggage for you, keep the most sentimental items and consider donating the rest to a person you actually know instead of to a large organization. Doing so may ease the process of letting go.

Swap Toys

Toy swaps provide unique opportunities for your children to acquire exciting, new-to-them toys without purchasing. Invite secondhand toys into your home by spearheading toy swaps with families in your community. It's as simple as hosting a playdate and asking mothers to bring over a handful of toys their children no longer play with. At the end of the playdate, make sure everyone leaves with different toys than they came with.

A friend in my community hosted a toy swap before the holidays and she created a wrapping station with wrapping paper, scissors, and tape. Mothers chose from the available toys and wrapped them there. Finding presents for their children was easy, free, and came with a bit of socializing.

If the idea of a toy swap sounds promising but your child isn't ready to permanently part with their toys, know that toy swaps also work well when you and another family agree to borrow instead of keep. Swap five toys with just one family, then swap back after a pre-determined period of time. This way, your child will receive new toys without the sense of loss that comes with giving toys up for good.

Be Artwork Savvy

Save the best of the best. For the rest, take photos of your child holding their artwork before responsibly discarding.

When Ani was a toddler I felt obligated to keep her best drawings and paintings. I envisioned giving each of my grown daughters a box that encapsulated the very best of their childhoods. I believed I owed it to them to diligently hold onto their earliest attempts at creativity.

But then I had a change of heart. My own sentimental box that my mother had dutifully saved for me had been sitting in the corner of my basement for years. One day I decided to open it and found my childhood artwork, report cards, school projects, and a smattering of photographs strewn inside. I spent hours combing through each item, and I desperately wanted to feel some sort of sentiment toward the contents inside. While the photographs solicited significant emotion, the piles of childhood artwork and school projects did not.

I decided to pare down my childhood box from an oversized, thirty-gallon tote to a curated collection of my childhood highlights. I saved photographs and a few pieces of writing I thought were particularly clever. But the rest felt like a burden. The little girl who painted those paintings and earned those grades didn't represent the woman I am today. I recycled what I could and discarded the rest.

These days, I adopt the same strategy with my daughters' artwork and school papers. I take care to remember that art is meant to be enjoyed, not stored in a box in the basement for the next eighteen years. Further, the joy of creating is a direct result of the creative process. My daughters do not draw for their future selves—they draw for their own enjoyment in the present moment.

As you tackle your child's artwork, save the best of the best by placing these items in their baby book. Hang the rest up and enjoy it for a short amount of time, then take a photograph of your child holding their work and send the physical art to a family member to enjoy.

For artwork destined for the garbage, remember to carefully remove three-dimensional elements like googly eyes and pipe cleaners and save them for future creative endeavors. Urge your child to create with crayons and colored pencils, as markers eventually become unnecessary plastic waste. Don't forget to reuse paper, too: keep a designated drawer or bin specifically for paper scraps. Preserve the brown filler paper from online orders, encourage your child to draw or paint on it, and then repurpose it into wrapping paper during the holiday season.

Common Concerns and How to Overcome Them

"My new baby received so many items that we'll never use. I feel guilty and overwhelmed."

Babies grow quickly, and they rarely wear all the new outfits or play with all the new toys. Return what you know you won't use and sell what you don't have receipts for. Give away what you can't return or sell, and try not to feel guilty about it. It's smarter to pass such items along to families who can and will use them than have them sit unused in a corner of your home. Use your guilt and overwhelm to inform your future gifting decisions for new parents and babies. Whenever you gift, consider giving what the *parents* need as opposed to what the *baby* needs. Bring over an entire dinner that includes salad, wine, entrée, and dessert, or contribute toward the price of a house cleaner. What most new parents need is help, not more baby clothes.

"I have tried talking to my family about our no-gifts wishes, but they keep gifting plastic toys anyway."

Many relatives have been over-gifters their entire lives and are unlikely to change their ways anytime soon. If nothing changed after an open and honest conversation about your parental preferences, enlist the help of a wish list. While wish lists work well in advance of holidays and birthdays, consider keeping a running list of items for the most ardent of givers. When you ask for specific and needed items, you empower your gift-giving relatives to be helpful while also limiting the potential for junk items.

"I desperately need to declutter my children's toys, but every time I try they put up legitimate fights."

It is often the case that older children bristle at the thought of parting with their toys. For particularly difficult toy decisions, consider removing some items temporarily. Encourage your child to fill a basket with items they are not yet ready to part with, and be sure to put as much in as needed to make your home's toy space feel tidy. Next, put that basket out of sight. Reserve these toys as rainy day back-ups for when your kids are restless and bored and need something "new" to play with. And if your children never ask for the contents of the back-up bin, you can feel confident about passing them on without a massive meltdown.

CHAPTER 5

Eco-Friendly Capsule Wardrobes

In my early days as a new mom, I had a closet full of nothing to wear. I owned countless garments from my previous teaching career—fancy blouses, slacks, skirts, and dresses. But I wasn't teaching anymore, and business casual attire was laughably impractical for my new life as a stay-at-home mom.

There were other clothes I never wore for different reasons: jeans that fit before I had children, shirts that heightened self-consciousness, and garments I received as gifts, but never liked and therefore never wore. I also spied a lot of fast fashion which, although once trendy, had already gone out of style. And because these fast fashion pieces were inexpensive, they looked drab and worn as they hung on their hangers.

Getting dressed was stress-inducing. On the days I stayed home, I cloaked myself in a dingy sweatshirt and yoga pants. On the rare occasions I went out, I tossed everything on my bed, crossed my fingers, and tried everything on until I found a single outfit that worked.

Advocates of capsule wardrobes argue that small, curated closets improve self-esteem, reduce mental overwhelm, and take the stress out of getting dressed. And while I considered creating one out of my existing closet for months, the idea just didn't make cognitive sense. How could having fewer clothes— and therefore, fewer choices—make getting dressed easier? Shouldn't I keep lots of clothes in order to have the best chance of looking my best?

It wasn't until I actually created a capsule wardrobe that I embraced its ingenuity. My own capsule reduced decision fatigue when getting dressed and eliminated guilt. The best part? Having a capsule wardrobe laid the foundation for improved shopping habits. I found myself viewing clothes as investment pieces, as opposed to disposable commodities.

I naturally adopted a slow fashion mindset that emphasized classic silhouettes, natural fibers, and quality craftsmanship.

Fast Fashion versus Slow Fashion

While wearers of fast fashion tend to view clothing as a disposable commodity, adopters of a slow fashion mindset treat garments as investments to be worn for years and years.

There are fundamental differences between fast fashion and slow fashion, and understanding the distinctions between the two greatly simplifies the decluttering process. While wearers of fast fashion tend to view clothing as a disposable commodity, adopters of a slow fashion mindset treat garments as investments to be worn for years and years.

Because fast fashion is defined by inexpensive price tags, cheap fabrics, and ultra-trendy silhouettes destined to go out of style by next season, the industry makes its profit from the constant turnover of product and contributes to textile waste and microfiber pollution. The toxins and pollutants created in manufacturing processes may not be properly disposed of and pollute streams, waterways, and soil.[52] And because fast fashion is so inexpensive, textile workers are often inadequately compensated for their labor.

Declutter Prepared

Although there are benefits to capsule wardrobes, the sad truth is that many attempts at paring closets down fail. Creating a *successful* capsule wardrobe requires deep understandings of both body type and fiber creation.

Know Your Body Type

Many consumers incorrectly assume that current fashion trends will flatter their figures. Emphasizing unique assets improves confidence, and dressing for shape empowers people to eliminate all the items in their closets that do not flatter. Before creating your capsule, it is crucial to first know and love your unique shape. Knowing your body type—which is dependent less on weight, and more on how your weight is proportioned on your body—enables you to selectively retain items that accentuate assets and donate ones that highlight flaws. While all bodies are unique, and some may not fit these classifications perfectly, most can identify with at least one of these shapes, to use as a guiding point when dressing themselves.

Female Body Types

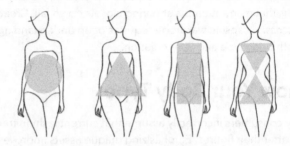

Understanding which garments flatter your body type (and which ones don't)
simplifies the closet decluttering process.

The Hourglass

Hourglass women consider themselves curvy. Their bust and
hips are roughly the same measurement and they have a well-
defined waist. If you have an hourglass shape, you will benefit
from emphasizing your midsection by wearing fitted tops, wrap
dresses, and anything with a belt.

The Pear

Bodies that boast wider hips than shoulders are considered
pear-shaped. Women who identify as pears benefit from
bringing attention to the top half of their silhouettes. If
you consider yourself a pear, focus on statement tops with
plunging necklines, bell sleeves, scoop necks, or cowl necks

that draw the eye upward. Wear bulky necklaces and flashy earrings to generate proportion, too.

The Rectangle

Women who have similar shoulder and hip measurements, but not a well-defined waist, are considered to be rectangles. Emphasize proportion by wearing loose-fitting tops with form-fitting bottoms. Similarly, wear halter-back and razorback tops to draw positive attention to your arms and shoulders.

The Apple

Apple shapes have wider shoulders than hips, often with a full bust. Apples benefit from abandoning clothing items with a structured waistline. Instead, focus on A-line dresses and tunics.

Male Body Types

The Inverted Triangle

Inverted triangles boast shoulders that are wider than their hips. Add bulk to your lower body to make it proportional to your upper half by focusing less on form-fitting pants and more on dark, looser-fitting denims, slim ties, and shoes with thicker soles.

The Oval

Ovals have torsos that are wider than their shoulders and hips.
They tend to have shorter and broader limbs, too. Add shape
to your frame by tucking in dress shirts with vertical stripes,
and seek out tapered bottoms in muted tones as a means of
trimming your silhouette.

The Rectangle

Rectangles tend to be tall, thin, and have shoulders that are
the same width as their hips. Add structure to your appearance
by wearing slim-cut pants, boldly patterned tops, and
tailored jackets.

Invest in Natural Fibers

Know exactly what your clothes are made of before
decluttering a single thing.

In order to make fabric, one needs thread. And to make thread,
one needs fibers. There are fundamental differences between
natural fibers, synthetic fibers, and semi-synthetic fibers, and
each have unique environmental implications. But while textile
corporations tout the words "eco-friendly" and "sustainable" to
describe their materials, they shadow manufacturing processes
from the public and obscure garment labels with hard-to-
understand terms. It is no surprise, then, that consumers
remain confused over what eco-friendly fibers are and why
they are important.

Natural Fibers

Derived from plants and animals, natural fibers are durable, eco-friendly, and lend themselves to high-quality garments.

Plants and animals produce natural fibers. Garments made from natural fibers are typically more comfortable, as they allow the skin to breathe, especially during warm or humid weather. They also tend to last longer than synthetics. Examples of natural fibers made from plants are cotton, hemp, and linen; examples of natural fibers made from animals are wool and silk.

Consumers adore **cotton**. Although cotton is a water-intensive crop, cotton clothing is absorbent, hypoallergenic, and quite soft, too. But not all cotton is created equal: while conventional cotton farming practices rely heavily on pesticides and insecticides, organic cotton is harvested without chemicals.

Because pesticides pollute soil and waterways, it is important from an environmental perspective to purchase cotton items made from 100-percent organic cotton. **Hemp**, by contrast, is an incredibly eco-friendly fiber because it grows quickly without chemicals and with very little water. It's also hypoallergenic and non-irritating to the skin. Hemp garments are scratchy when purchased new, but they age well—the more you wash hemp, the softer it becomes.

Linen is a natural fiber made from flax plants. Linen absorbs and releases water quickly, so the fabric continues to feel cool and dry to the touch even in hot, humid weather. Linen is lint-free, softens the more you wash it, and is very durable. But because it has low elasticity, it's often used for looser-fitting styles.

Wool and silk are two natural fibers made from animals. Humans have relied on wool for centuries as a natural insulator that is wrinkle-free, hypoallergenic, and absorbs harmful pollutants. Silk, by contrast, is spun from the long threads that make up the inner cocoon of a silkworm. The fibers are in fact saliva, produced by the worm to insulate itself until it is time to transform. Raw silk threads are harvested and reeled together for commercial use.

Synthetic Fibers

If a garment is stretchy, shiny, waterproof, lightweight or wrinkle-free, synthetic fibers probably make it so. Synthetic fibers are made by humans through chemical synthesis, and although synthetic fibers account for more than 60 percent of textile fibers used in the world, they contribute significantly to microplastic pollution when washed in our washing machines. **Nylon, polyester, spandex, Lycra, and acrylic** are examples of synthetic fibers.

Polyester is the world's most popular synthetic fiber. Indeed, polyester is well-loved by consumers because it is wrinkle-free, dries quickly, and often inexpensive. But polyester is melted plastic that is squeezed through a spinneret to create long, continuous filaments. As you wash your polyester clothing, these filaments break down, enter waterways, and contribute to microplastic pollution. A single garment may shed up to 1,900 fibers every time it's washed.[53] And, as is the problem with all plastics, synthetic fibers are not biodegradable and persist in our ecosystems even as they break apart. While high-quality polyester clothing can last for a long time, the vast majority of polyester on the market is cheap, poor-quality, fast fashion, which will last only few wears before breaking down.

Semi-Synthetic Fibers

Semi-synthetic fibers are man-made plant fibers. Although semi-synthetics are *derived* from plants, some demand the use of harsh chemicals during the fiber creation process. **Rayon and viscose** are two semi-synthetic fibers made from bamboo. Bamboo is the fastest-growing plant in the world that does not require chemical fertilizers or pesticides; it requires four times less water than cotton, too. But transforming bamboo into soft, fuzzy fabrics requires chemicals, which are often improperly disposed of and thus pollute waterways.[54]

Eucalyptus creates soft and wrinkle-free fibers, and **TENCEL's lyocell and modal** are semi-synthetic fibers derived from the eucalyptus tree. These semi-synthetic fibers do not necessarily require harmful chemicals, as factory workers utilize a safer chemical during production. They do not discharge it into waterways, either.[55]

Which fibers should consumers keep when decluttering their closets? While lyocell and modal are more eco-friendly than viscose or rayon, they are not as sustainable as natural fibers like linen and hemp. If you must buy a semi-synthetic fiber, know that Tencel is considered to be the most eco-friendly fabric of all the semi-synthetics.

Real Life Sustainable Minimalists

Simplified Closet, Simplified Life

I created my capsule wardrobe by accident. I'm extremely overwhelmed and anxious on a daily basis, and given that I've struggled with dressing myself my entire life, I decided that the closet seemed like an ideal place to start simplifying. After a few iterations of tweaking my wardrobe to make it more cohesive, it dawned on me that I had, in fact, created a capsule wardrobe.

This first foray into simplifying changed my life and I saw immediate, vast improvements in my mental health. My confidence sky-rocketed and my daily attitude improved.

Getting dressed has become so simple, and I no longer waste time trying to decide what to wear. Because everything matches, I pull items out of my closet and go. I save time, reduce decision fatigue, and feel confident throughout the day. I've also enjoyed the benefit of doing less laundry. There's less to wash, less to fold, and less to put away.

Shopping has now become an adventure: instead of walking into a huge box store and being overwhelmed by all the choices, knowing exactly what I need to round out my wardrobe makes it much easier to focus on finding the right quality pieces instead of getting distracted by what's trendy.

Creating a capsule wardrobe was a gateway to simplifying my life as a whole. Once I decluttered my closet, I couldn't stop myself from simplifying all other areas of my life. My anxiety has disappeared thanks to living simply, and it all traces back to my capsule wardrobe.

Amanda Warfield, episodes #072 and #079 podcast guest
amandawarfield.com

Creating Your Capsule Wardrobe

Separate your clothing and accessories into four distinct categories: Keep, Donate, Mend, and Repurpose.

A successful capsule wardrobe must first be decluttered. But garments often garner conflicting emotions, and purging wardrobes can be a difficult task. Those jeans may usher in shame at the realization they no longer fit (and have not in a long time). And that expensive dress? To some, it may represent a wasted paycheck.

The good news is that getting dressed can be a calmer and more joyful process after clearing out the clutter with the Four-Box System. Arm yourself with four oversized boxes or bins and label them Keep, Donate, Mend, and Repurpose.

Items to Keep

Discern slow fashion items from their fast fashion counterparts by reserving slow fashion pieces that are made from natural fibers and boast classic silhouettes. Keep clothes that accent your unique body type, too, and match the other items you have chosen to keep. The internet overflows with advice on creating successful capsule wardrobes, but I believe that much of this advice complicates the task unnecessarily. Simply choose items in neutral hues that match when worn together.

If you're worried that your decluttered wardrobe is too monochromatic, intentionally keep two or three bold or patterned items. Remember that, while a few garments with vivid prints and textures add intrigue, too many outliers will result in all of them being unworn.

Your Capsule's Parameters

5 neutral tops (black, white, grey, navy blue)
6 neutral bottoms
2 neutral dresses
5 accent (patterned) tops
5 accent (patterned) bottoms
2 accent (patterned) dresses
A few accent pieces, including hats, scarves, cardigans, and vests
Total: 30 to 50 pieces

Items to Donate

Donate items that are ultra-trendy but not your style, don't flatter your body type, or don't currently fit. Consider donating items made of delicate, dry-clean only fabrics, too, as dry cleaning relies on harsh chemicals, and frequent exposure to such chemicals can quickly degrade fabrics. Because donation centers are overwhelmed with the sheer amount of fast fashion items consumers drop off every single day, it's prudent to remember the cardinal rule of donating: only donate items in very good condition. If an item is ripped, stained, torn, stretched, or otherwise shabby, place it in the Repurpose box instead.

If after you declutter your closet, you realize that your Donate pile is significantly larger than your other piles, you may have invested heavily into fast fashion. Let the process of decluttering your wardrobe inform your future purchasing decisions, and when the time comes to acquire new clothes, use the suggestions I've listed at the end of the chapter to help you add to your wardrobe in a sustainable manner.

Items to Repurpose

Reserve stained, torn, and stretched items from your closet for repurposing. Less-than-pristine clothing should not be donated to a traditional donation center, but it is entirely possible to repurpose the fabric into new, useful items. If you have children, repurpose some fancier garments into dress-up clothes and cut bold, patterned pieces into scraps for future arts and crafts projects.

The simplest repurposing idea is to reserve clothes made from natural fibers and cut them neatly into squares, then reuse them in place of napkins and paper towels in your home. Roll and place them decoratively in a basket. Alternately, keep your counter clear by laying rags flat in a drawer. Over time you may find cotton rags to be much more absorbent than paper, and you may also enjoy the added savings of no longer buying napkins and paper towels.

Use Your Sewing Machine Skills

If you are skilled with a sewing machine, the opportunities for repurposing old clothes are endless. Some ideas include:

- Quilts and pillowcases
- Totes and produce bags
- Draft stoppers (to stop cold air from entering under doors and windows)
- Hair accessories
- Doll clothes
- Table runners
- Wall hangings

Find yourself reserving many blemished garments, but have no desire to repurpose them yourself? Some communities have textile donation centers that accept ripped, stained clothing. Such donation centers will repurpose your garments into filling for pillows and stuffed animals, or into industrial rags. Inquire as to whether your community has a local textile recycling program for items that are too shabby to be conventionally donated. Alternately, know that Goodwill accepts damaged fabric items and will recycle them appropriately on your behalf. Help Goodwill employees by pre-sorting: separate clothes to be recycled from clothes you are donating and label them accordingly.

Items to Mend

Our grandparents and great-grandparents cared for their clothing. They tended to imperfections because fabric was expensive, and mending was therefore a way of life. But because the fast fashion industry has lowered clothing prices to the point where garments are essentially disposable, consumers revere new clothes, even when such items are poorly made. And because fast fashion is so inexpensive, consumers often trash garments with ripped elbows or torn sleeves without remorse.

Easy clothing repairs without a sewing machine include mending a torn seam, patching a big or small hole, adding buttons, and hiding snags. Put items that require small fixes aside and vow to tackle them later by watching free tutorials online.

If a garment requires a bigger fix like replacing a zipper, hemming, or taking it in, ask yourself whether someone in your life knows how to fix these imperfections and will let you watch and learn. Remember your local tailor and support a small business by bringing in mending jobs that require professional expertise.

Caring for Your Capsule

Preserving what you already have is an intentional practice that reduces waste, saves money, and fights back against a disposability mindset. Use the following tried-and-true techniques to extend the life of your existing capsule:

Act Quickly on Stains

Prevent spills from becoming stains by carrying a stain removal pen, then wash the garment immediately upon arriving home. To remove lipstick stains, spray the fabric with hairspray and let it sit for a few minutes, then dab the stain and toss non-dry cleaning fabrics in the washing machine. For grease stains, cover the entire stain with clear dish detergent and rub it in with your fingers or an old toothbrush. Then rinse out the detergent, add white vinegar, rinse again after three minutes, and wash as normal.

Fix Shoe Problems

Hide scuffs on patent leather with a cotton swab and some petroleum jelly. Scrub out water stains on leather with an old toothbrush and a bit of vinegar. Finally, clean stubborn dirt from suede by lightly rubbing the stain with a nail file.

Wash and Dry Smarter

Before washing, turn some items inside-out, including shirts with graphics and garments with bright colors. Do not overload your washing machine, either, as that increases the chances of clothes rubbing against one another and subsequently degrading more quickly than in a properly filled machine. Because denim is a rough material, wash jeans in their own load to keep them separate from delicate fabrics.

Use less detergent, as too much fades clothes, adheres to fabrics, and makes items appear stiff. Wash your clothes in cold water for both the health of your garments and for the health of the planet—roughly 90 percent of the energy spent washing clothes is attributed to heating the water in the machine.[56] Washing clothes in water that is sixty degrees Fahrenheit as compared to seventy-five degrees Fahrenheit can save you $60 annually in utilities.[57]

Finally, avoid the dryer. High heat quickly ages fibers, and shrinks and fades clothing. If you must use the dryer, skip the single-use dryer sheets and use a dryer ball instead. A wool dryer ball increases the efficacy of the dryer because it retains heat, reduces overall drying time, and prevents laundry from clumping in the dryer.

Adding to Your Capsule

Now that you've thinned out your wardrobe, what's next? For many, the process of wardrobe decluttering is a transformative one, and a slow fashion mindset often replaces one that once bought into fast fashion.

Still, clothing is a necessity, and you will find yourself needing to add to your wardrobe in the future. But purchasing new clothes creates unnecessary pollution and waste. Indeed, although accessible, clean water amounts to less than 1 percent of the world's water supply, the manufacturing of a single cotton T-shirt demands 713 gallons.[58] Instead of purchasing new items, consider investing in quality secondhand 90 percent of the time, and buy new just 10 percent of the time. Here are some ways you can sustainably add to your wardrobe.

Thrift

Purchasing secondhand sends a powerful message to retailers that you're uninterested in introducing additional products to the market. Savvy, modern thrifters look beyond brick-and-mortar storefronts. They frequent websites instead, and use sites' search parameters to find an exact item in their desired color and size for a fraction of a new item's price. I offer my best secrets for twenty-first century thrifting in chapter 9.

Rent

There once was a time in my life when I bought a new dress for each occasion I was invited to. The result was a closet full of dresses and gowns that were barely worn and out of style. I've since adopted the belief that it's smarter to purchase a single dress that can be styled up or down depending on the occasion than to buy dozens of dresses destined to be worn just once.

Sometimes it makes sense to rent a particular garment than to buy new, too. If you have a formal event on your calendar, consider renting your attire. **Renttherunway.com** and **Armoire.style** offer luxurious pieces in many styles and sizes for a fraction of their market cost.

Swap with Friends

Clothing swaps save money, reduce textile waste, and lower swappers' carbon footprints. They are also enjoyable ways to socialize with friends. Simply invite your friends over and ask them to bring clothes and accessories they no longer wear. Once everyone arrives, enlist everyone's help in organizing garments into distinct, categorical piles (tops, bottoms, skirts, scarves, etc.). Then invite guests to sift through and find items to try on and perhaps take home.

If you prefer a less structured way to swap clothes, simply swap items with a friend whose size and style are similar to your own.

Accept Heirloom Pieces

If you are fortunate enough to have family members offering to pass down heirloom clothes and jewelry, consider accepting them, so long as there's a high probability you'll wear them. Doing so may infuse a timeless quality to your wardrobe while also memorializing your loved ones.

When You Do Buy New...

If you are financially able, seek out garments that are made of 100-percent natural fibers, that accentuate your body type, and that are sold by eco-friendly and ethical manufacturers. I have listed some brands for men, women, and children in the appendix of this book. Be sure to read garment labels, too: it's often the case that a garment advertising natural fibers neglects to mention that a percentage of the item is also made with synthetics.

Common Concerns and How to Overcome Them

"My closet has a lot of fast fashion pieces, and now I feel guilty. What should I do with them all?"

Provided the items still fit and you still like them, wear them over and over again. The most eco-friendly action is to wear what you already have.

"Is it ever ethical to buy fast fashion?"

Ethical fashion can be pricey. But as we've discussed, fast fashion can be even more so when you think about CPW. If your financial means enable you to support ethical and sustainable retailers, forego fast fashion altogether. If, however, financial or other limitations prevent you from supporting ethical companies, consider thrifting quality pieces instead of buying fast fashion that's new.

"I live in a cold weather climate. I'm worried that if I declutter too much, I'll be unprepared for the change in seasons."

I live in a cold weather climate with four very distinct seasons. In order to be ready for the changes in weather, I have four capsule wardrobes. I keep the current season's wardrobe in my closet, and I store the remaining three bins on my closet's top shelf.

PART 2

Sustainability and the Middle of the Tree

CHAPTER 6

Your Low-Waste Kitchen

Low-waste kitchens are mindful of energy, water, food, and packaging waste.

A lifestyle rooted in eco-friendliness extends far beyond a single responsible declutter, and that's because sustainability encompasses many planet-first habits that, when practiced concurrently, define a lifestyle. Reducing waste, minimizing your carbon footprint, supporting your local economy, adopting natural and homemade products, lowering environmental toxins, and becoming self-sufficient are all pillars of a sustainable mindset. In parts 2 and 3 of this book, we will tackle these facets of sustainability one by one, and we'll start with reducing waste.

Thanks to food packaging, paper products, and scraps from uneaten meals, American kitchens create an awful lot of trash.

The rise of individually wrapped food options—like potato chips in miniature cellophane bags, single-serve cheese sticks wrapped in plastic sleeves, and raisins within plastic-lined boxes—has substantially increased the amount of trash that homes produce. Citing convenience, corporations market individually wrapped products to over-worked and time-crunched adults. Yet few consumers realize such items at the supermarket are almost always more expensive—and more environmentally detrimental—than their bulk-packaged counterparts.

Single-use items like paper napkins, plastic plates, paper towels, and plastic cutlery have also overtaken many twenty-first century kitchens. And because the fossil fuel and plastic industries are uniquely intertwined, they are poised to mutually benefit from a single-use society. Over 99 percent of plastic is made from chemicals sourced from fossil fuels like coal, oil, and gas.[59] Fossil fuels release carbon dioxide into the air when burned, which significantly contributes to global warming. Worse, just as the general public has begun to grasp the dangers of plastic pollution and climate change, both the fossil fuel and plastic industries are planning to *expand* plastic production in the coming decades.[60]

Curbing climate change also means reducing waste, and the most wasteful room in many homes tends to be the kitchen.

Zero-Waste?

The zero-waste movement educates the public on critical issues surrounding disposability. And while sending less garbage to the landfill is certainly a pillar of sustainability, an expansive definition of waste includes wasted energy, water, fossil fuels, minerals, and more. When you analyze the problem through a wide lens instead of a narrow one, true zero-waste living likely seems unrealistic.

Let's say you just purchased a new cotton T-shirt. Even if you left the plastic hanger with the clerk and placed your purchase in your reusable tote bag, you'd be incorrect in assuming that your purchase created zero waste. That's because, before that T-shirt arrived at the store, a garment worker wrapped it in a plastic bag, lumped it together with other shirts in a bigger plastic bag, and then placed into a cardboard box for shipment. Other waste beyond physical garbage was likely created during production and manufacturing, too, like wasted water when growing the cotton, wasted energy during manufacturing, and wasted manufacturing byproducts that became pollution. Forgoing a new shirt and buying one secondhand would create similar waste—albeit significantly less—because you generated carbon emissions by driving to the thrift store or by having it shipped to your doorstep after it buying online.

Almost all environmental problems result from waste.

Globally, humans transform over one hundred billion tons of raw material, including minerals, ores, fossil fuels, and biomass, into products or food each year.[61] Yet two-thirds of it all becomes waste. Waste is trash in oceans and garbage in landfills, yes, but waste is also uneaten food, lost manufacturing byproducts, and even pollution.

Almost all environmental problems result from waste. And while the idea of a circle economy is gaining international traction as a means of wasting nothing on an international scale, I believe each of us can adopt the tenets of a circular economy within our own homes by making conscious choices aimed at reducing *all* forms of waste.

The Three-Bin System for Waste Collection

Reduce food waste and send as little to the landfill each week by utilizing three distinct bins to separate waste. Your three bins will include a recycling bin, a small compost transport container, and a bin for trash that cannot otherwise be recycled or composted.

1. A Recycling Bin

While many consumers put anything and everything into the recycling bin in the hopes that these items will magically be recycled, this practice often creates more harm than good.

Non-recyclables clog machinery, take extra time to sort, and make the recycling process more difficult for municipalities around the world.

Pragmatic recycling starts by understanding that not all towns collect the same materials. Designate a bin specifically for items that *can* be recycled, per your municipality's guidelines. Look up your town or city's recycling rules on its website, then help your family by creating a recycle cheat-sheet and pasting it to the side of the bin. Keep your kitchen recycling bin unlined, as the lining creates waste. Make sure to wash and dry any containers before recycling them to increase their chances of actually get recycled.

All Plastics Are Not Created Equal

The Society of Plastics Industry established plastic recycling symbols in 1988.[62] Each number within the triangle logo corresponds to specific resins in the material. While some resins are easily recycled, others are not.

#1 Polyethylene terephthalate (PET) is used to make soda bottles, water bottles, and many other liquid containers, and is one of the most commonly recycled plastics in the United States.

#2 High density polyethylene (HDPE), a commonly recycled plastic, is used to make containers for cleaning products and milk.

#3 Polyvinyl chloride (PVC) is used to make plastic pipes and some liquid containers. It is not commonly recycled.

#4 Low density polyethylene (LDPE) creates plastic bags, plastic wrap, and some squeezable bottles. It is not commonly recycled.

#5 Polypropylene (PP) is used to make bottle caps, prescription bottles, and other hard plastic containers. It is not commonly recycled.

#6 Polystyrene (PS) is better known as Styrofoam and is rarely recycled.

#7 This miscellaneous category includes all resins not defined by other groups. They are not commonly recycled.

---

2. Composting Essentials

Your transport container reserves food scraps until you've collected enough to warrant a schlep to your outdoor tumbler.

Because landfills are devoid of light and air, food scraps do not decompose properly in them. Instead, they produce methane as they break down, which contributes to global warming. Composting at home drastically reduces the amount of trash your household produces and is also a powerful way to do your part to curb warming gases. While we discuss how exactly to compost in chapter 10, we will set up your compost system now.

If you live in a small space without a yard, know that you, too, can compost by either doing so indoors or by contributing to a municipal program. Purchase a vermicomposting or bokashi kit instead of a transport container and tumbler, both of which facilitate the creation of indoor compost. Alternately, municipal composting is gaining traction, especially in cities. Inquire as to whether your city or town will take food scraps from your curb.

If you have a bit of yard space, setting up your composting essentials requires that you acquire two tools by thrifting, repurposing, or buying new: a transport container and an outdoor compost tumbler.

A Transport Container

A small transport container reserves food scraps in your kitchen until you've collected enough to warrant making a schlep to the outdoor tumbler. It is small (approximately 1–1.5 gallons) and ideally resides out of sight. I keep my transport container under my sink.

When I first started composting, I refused to purchase a transport container and instead repurposed an old yogurt tub. Because it had a lid, I kept it covered to prevent smells from wafting into my kitchen. But because it was just quart-sized, it filled quickly. I found myself running to my outdoor compost bin more often than fit into my busy life.

Next, I repurposed a milk jug by cutting off the top just above the handle. While I appreciated the jug's larger size, I bemoaned the fact that it didn't have a cover. It had an unpleasant smell that wafted into the kitchen whenever I went too long without emptying it.

Then I purchased the cheapest transport container online. While it was large and had a lid, it wasn't lined with a compostable bag. Cleaning it was therefore a frequent, unpleasant task. Over time, I was unable to get it fully clean.

If your transport container is too small, you'll find yourself running to your outside bin more often than you'd like. If it's too big, it will likely become an eyesore. My journey to find the right compost container has convinced me that it is prudent to acquire a quality transport container at the outset because doing so eliminates unnecessary hassles, limits setbacks as you attempt to foster a new habit, and improves the chances that your efforts will stick. Measure the location where you plan to put your transport bin and buy one that fits in that allocated space. Remember, too, that airflow is everyone's friend. Although decomposition should not happen in your transport container, a lack of oxygen forces food scraps to decompose quicker. Find a transport container that boasts breathability and is also lidded, as lids keep out smells and potential household critters.

A Tumbler

Composting's second essential tool is an outdoor compost bin. The outdoor compost bin is large (at least thirty gallons) and is where the actual breakdown of food scraps occurs. While there are many outdoor composting products on the market, I find the tumbler to be the easiest and most fool-proof option. Compost must be turned every few weeks. You can either do this yourself with a bit of elbow grease and a shovel, or you can purchase a compost bin that turns your compost for you. By choosing a tumbler at the outset, you will never have to manually turn your compost pile.

Want to repurpose what you already have instead of buying new? It's entirely possible to make your own outdoor compost bin—though not a tumbler—by repurposing a lidded, forty-gallon plastic bin. Find one that's at least twenty-four inches in height, then drill ten holes in the bottom for aeration. Line the bottom of the inside with dry leaves and newspaper, then fill it halfway with dirt.

Place your tumbler or bin in an optimal location outdoors. Choose a spot that is close enough to a household exit so walking to it once per day is not an inconvenient schlep, yet far enough away so it's not an eyesore. Make sure the space you have chosen gets plenty of sun—the composting process requires heat, so a sunny spot will create compost quicker than a shaded one.

3. A Trash Bin

Low-waste kitchens orbit around a singular goal: send as little as possible to the landfill each week.

When we first became conscious of our trash production, Haig and I found ourselves motivated to reduce by tracking our progress in a non-fancy and unofficial notebook. We reduced our usual weeks' worth of trash from two full bags to just one. In time—and with very little effort!—we dropped our pickup schedule to every other week.

There is nothing special about a trash can, and you likely already have one in your kitchen. In a perfect world, your kitchen's trash bin is small (because you create very little trash!) and is lined with anything other than a plastic bag, such as newspaper or a repurposed paper bag.

Real Life Sustainable Minimalists

Weigh That Waste

My family reduced our household waste by thirty-five pounds a week (yes, I weighed it). The biggest area of improvement for us was the kitchen. The kitchen was the largest source of waste in our home and reducing its trash seemed overwhelming. I didn't know where to start, and I realized we needed to first know what we were regularly throwing away. I identified three of the most common items in our bin, which were single-use paper towels, food packaging, and food waste.

My husband and I brainstormed ideas to start reducing. I created an "Eat Me Now" section in our refrigerator to reduce food waste. Now I can easily see what needs to be used up, which prevents items from going bad in the depths of the fridge.

I also knew composting was in our future, but I was scared to try. Luckily, composting proved to be a lot easier than I imagined! I constructed a backyard compost bin out of a tall hamper I found on the side of the road. I collect food scraps in a small mixing bowl on our counter. To reduce odors, we also reserve compost in the refrigerator or freezer until it's ready to be taken outside.

Swapping single-use paper towels for cloth was a swap I wasn't sure we were going to stick with; it just seemed unsanitary to use cloth on certain messes. However, after upcycling old burp cloths, stained towels, and other textiles into cleaning cloths, I can say we've never looked back! We keep a container of clean towels under our sink and we have another small bin for the dirty ones. Once it's full, I throw them in the washing machine.

To combat our own food packaging waste, we garden during non-winter months. When we do come home with packaging, I try to reuse it. I save and reuse bread and tortilla bags, and I use mushroom containers and plastic clamshells for starting seeds, too.

Laura Durenberger, episodes #020, #039, and #087
podcast guest

reducereuserenewblog.com

Reassessing Single-Use

It's less about uniformity: mismatched (but repurposed!) jars of varying sizes line this pantry.

The market economy reveres newness. These days, while many millennials and generation Y-ers harbor a new-is-best mindset, generations past had ingrained a "reuse" mindset well before zero-waste and low-waste living were popular. Thriftiness was a way of life for our grandparents and great-grandparents, and they boldly reused countless household items so that nothing valuable became waste.

Sustainable minimalism is mismatched and repurposed.

A commitment to low-waste living isn't about investing in perfectly uniform mason jars that line the pantry. It isn't about purchasing immaculate stainless steel reusables with cutesy labels, either. Sustainable minimalism is mismatched and repurposed. It's adorably threadbare rags, reused pickle jars that now hold lentils, and decades-old quality utensils and appliances. A low-waste lifestyles uses what you *already have* until it breaks or runs out, as repairing, repurposing, and reusing are the sustainable minimalist way.

Consider the following kitchen items with infinite reuse potential:

Aluminum Foil

A single sheet of aluminum foil can be used again and again to line pans, cover dishes, and wrap food items. After use, simply wash and lay flat to dry, then reuse as you would a new piece.

When foil becomes too wrinkled to reuse, repurpose it in place of a scouring pad by crushing it into a pancake and scrubbing grime off pots and pans. Alternately, harness its power to polish your silver: simply line a glass pan with the foil, pour in boiling water, add 1 tablespoon of baking soda, then add the silver.

Aluminum foil is very easily recycled, but you must first clean it. Be sure to wipe away food residue and grease before recycling.

Glass Jars

I am a proud jar maximalist and have a swoon-worthy collection of glass jars in varying sizes on hand at all times. Jars ensure both organization and tidiness, and thanks to their well-fitting lids, they keep food fresh, too. While I rely on mason jars again and again when canning and preserving food, I repurpose jars from the supermarket for organization in nearly every room in my home.

Utilize jars for food storage. Store leftover broths, soups, sauces, and condiments in jars in your refrigerator. Separate grains and loose-leaf tea, as well as pantry staples like lentils, grains, beans, and popcorn kernels into respective jars, too, and be sure to clearly label them. Make your own spice jars by storing home-grown, dried spices in small jars and poking holes in the lids. Pre-sort all the dry ingredients for cookies and brownies into jars, then store them in your pantry. Doing so will offer the convenience of boxed baked goods without the excess packaging.

Repurpose Those Jars!

A jar's utility extends beyond the kitchen. Here are additional ways to repurpose glass jars:

- In the bathroom, organize hair ties, cotton swabs, and bobby pins into jars.

- Reduce plastic waste associated with a liquid pump bottle by placing a repurposed soap pump atop a mason jar filled with liquid soap.

- Store homemade beauty products, including body lotion and dry shampoo, in smaller-sized jars.

- Organize desks, garages, laundry rooms, and more by using jars to separate nails, screws, paper clips, buttons, and safety pins.

- Pack lunch in a jar.

- Plant an indoor herb garden in wide-rimmed jars. Place rocks at the bottom for adequate water drainage, then add soil and your herb of choice.

- Utilize jars in craft products, including homemade beeswax candles, flower vases, and more.

If you have a stubborn label on a jar that you'd like to remove, simply mix one tablespoon of olive oil with one tablespoon of baking soda, then spread the mixture on the label and leave it be for two hours before rinsing it clean. Alternately, if you have a smelly jar, pour in a solution of equal parts vinegar and water to the top, then let it sit overnight with the lid off. Rinse it dry and store with the lid off.

Butter Wrappers

Purchase sticks of butter over butter in a plastic tub. Doing so eliminates wasteful disposal of that plastic container. The practice also empowers you to no longer buy cooking spray. Butter at room temperature will stick to its paper when removed. I store these butter papers in my refrigerator and use one to grease a pan before baking. A second way to grease pans without aerosol cooking spray is to simply arm yourself with a kitchen brush and "paint" the bottom of a pan with a bit of olive oil.

Eggshells

Eggshells give much-needed calcium to plants and deter insects. Simply crush shells using a mortar and pestle, then mix the crushed shells into soil of your plants.

Bread Tags

Bread tags facilitate cord organization. If you have a tangled cord pile, write the name of the cord's gadget on a bread tag (e.g., "alarm clock") then affix it to the correct cord. Make sure the label is facing outward so you can easily read it.

Cereal Box Liners

You can reuse the plastic bags inside cereal boxes in countless ways. Have a dog? Take one with you on your walks to pick up its fecal matter. Alternately, you can freeze food in cereal box liners. Simply put the food in the bag, then tie and tape it tightly shut, taking care to remove all the air inside. If you like to sew, tear apart the plastic cereal box liners at the seams, wipe them down, cut off where they were glued together, and then use the pieces for patterns. Lay your pattern piece under the plastic, then trace with a black sharpie.

The Slow Food Movement

Eating out is expensive, but cooking meals at home saves money and reduces plastic waste. Planning dinners ahead of time slashes food waste, too.

While it used to be that families convened nightly around the dinner table, these days families often eat on-the-go. Yet some of my own happiest childhood memories occurred around my grandmother's dinner table. Some days I helped her in the kitchen, others I set the table. My mother had a strict "finish your dinner" rule, and my grandmother would quietly sneak food from my plate when my mother wasn't looking. There was never an end-time to these family dinners, either—no one checked their watches under the table or, worse, their mobile phones. As afternoons rolled into evenings and the sun lowered itself just behind the trees, my mother would stand up. That's when my sister and I knew it was time to go.

Consider adopting a slow food mindset in your home as an alternative to the twenty-first century hustle and bustle. Make the act of gathering around the dinner table the highlight of your weekends as you slow down all the tasks related to creating a family meal. Explicitly teach your child how food grows as you water your backyard garden. Make trips to the farmer's market and enlist the family's help as you preserve fresh produce for the upcoming dormant season. And as you prepare those dinners, ask for your child's input. Cooking with your child teaches the importance of food and encourages better dietary habits.[63]

Incorporate Reusables

Low-waste kitchens rely on reusable items to quietly hum along. You may believe (as many consumers do) that single-use items are the convenient choices because they save time, but the reality is that you don't benefit in the long run from harboring a single-use mindset. Purchasing the same products over and over again depletes your wallet, trashes the planet, and pads the pockets of already wealthy corporate executives. And although disposability may have infiltrated your kitchen, know that it is absolutely possible to reacquaint yourself with reusable products in the forms of cloth napkins, metal straws, beeswax wraps, and more.

Use up what you already have, then invest in an eco-friendly alternative the next time you have to stock up. Eleven essential reusables in every low-waste kitchen include the following:

Water Bottles

Although many have safe drinking water, consumers have fallen into the habit of buying bottled water. But when we pay for an item that is free, we *actually* pay for the plastic packaging. Collectively, humans around the world pay for—and subsequently dispose of—one million plastic bottles per minute.[64]

Investing in a quality reusable water bottle made of glass or aluminum will save one hundred plastic bottles from the landfill each year.[65] [66] Keep one reusable water bottle in your kitchen per person in your household and fill them before leaving home.

Rags

My daughters (and pets) can make incredible messes. Still, I have found that there is rarely a mess that can't be wiped up by a good, old-fashioned rag.

Whereas paper towels cost money, rags are free. Rip up old towels and clothing items that are too worn to donate and store them under the kitchen sink. Reach for a rag next time you find yourself cleaning up a mess, then rinse it out before putting in the washing machine with the rest of your laundry.

Cloth Napkins

It is never the case that a single paper napkin suffices. Many times, each diner requires two or even three paper napkins in a single meal.

Instead of cutting down trees to wipe mouths, consider repurposing old clothes, sheets, and towels into cloth napkins. Reusable napkins perform their utility infinitely better than paper and can last for more than a single meal. For most meals, my family uses the non-fancy cloth napkins I made. But when we have guests over for dinner, I pull out the linen set.

Silicone Baking Mats and Muffin Liners

I love to bake, and I used to waste an awful lot of parchment paper. I have since swapped out parchment paper for silicone baking mats because a silicone mat replaces both parchment paper and greasy sprays. They're durable and infinitely reusable, too. Similarly, silicone muffin liners perform all the essential duties of paper liners, but without the waste. Invest in a single set and use them for decades.

Silicone, Plastic, or Neither?

Silicone is a compound comprised primarily of inert silicone (or sand) and oxygen, and sustainable minimalists often rely on silicone products in the kitchen because they boast low toxicity and high heat resistance.[67] Because silicone is incredibly durable and doesn't degrade, it is considered more eco-friendly than plastic. Many consumers appreciate that silicone is dishwasher and oven-safe, too.

Yet silicone isn't perfect—it is difficult to recycle and is rarely accepted by municipal recycling programs. And then there's the fact that silicone products are still products, and purchasing them unnecessarily constitutes unconscious consumerism. In this and all cases, let the Rs of eco-friendliness inform your purchasing decisions: reuse what you already have, repurpose another item for a new purpose, and refuse to buy items you don't need, even if they seem eco-friendly.

If you do invest in silicone cookware, look for items made from food grade or medical grade silicone that do not contain fillers.

Silicone Bags

Reusable bags can replace Ziplocks and come in various sizes, from snack-sized to quart and gallon. Although many companies sell reusable bags, many of them are made from a thicker plastic. Consider investing in a brand that boasts bags made of silicone, even though they may be more expensive than their plastic counterparts.

Beeswax Wraps

Beeswax wraps are the eco-friendly alternative to plastic wrap, as they can be reused over and over again for years to come. While many companies sell beeswax wraps, it is also entirely possible to make them at home. Simply Google "homemade beeswax wraps" for countless tutorials.

French Press

Single-serve coffee machines waste enormous amounts of plastic, and most drip machines require single-use filters. French presses, on the other hand, enable coffee lovers to brew without waste. Many find that French press coffee also tastes best because, while drip machines absorb much of the oil found in coffee grounds, a French press enables grounds to steep barrier-free. Know, however, that five to eight cups of unfiltered coffee per day may raise your LDL cholesterol, so make sure to keep an eye on your cholesterol levels over time.[68]

Metal Straws

While many households happily function without straws whatsoever, both young children and those with disabilities often rely on the convenience that straws offer. Consider swapping out plastic straws with metal ones, and find a set that includes a small cleaning brush so they remain sanitary for the long haul.

Lidded Glass Containers in Varying Sizes

Plastic Tupperware stains, retains odors, and warps over time. Research also suggests that when such containers are heated the chemicals within—which are linked to metabolic disorders and reduced fertility—leach into food.[69] My family prefers glass containers, and I've collected dozens in various sizes over the years. I use them to store leftovers in the refrigerator, freeze food for later, pack snacks for my children's lunches, and purchase various food items at the grocery store.

Bamboo Dish Brush

Replace unsanitary sponges with a bamboo dish brush with an interchangeable head. Alternately, scrub dishes with a rag, wash it in the washing machine, and use it again and again.

Glass Spice Jars

Spices retain their potency for just six months before losing flavor. Buying spices in plastic at the supermarket creates excess waste in both the plastic container as well as the unused product. A smarter option is to purchase fresh and package-free spices in the quantity you need, then store them at home in your own glass jars. While you can certainly buy a uniform set of glass spice jars, reusing baby food jars also works well.

Tackle Energy Waste

It is often the case that low-wasters get so caught up in the challenge of garbage reduction that they overlook other ways in which their actions harm the planet. Committing to sustainability is not *just* about reducing household trash. It's about reducing carbon footprints, too, as carbon emissions are directly responsible for global warming and climate change.

Your carbon footprint is the total amount of greenhouse gases your actions generate within one year. While the global average is about four tons per person, the average carbon footprint for an American is sixteen tons in a single year.[70] And while many associate carbon emissions with automobiles—driving does indeed increase one's footprint—your carbon footprint is affected by household activities including heating, cooling, and overall electricity use. Conscious changes in the kitchen will lower your carbon footprint, reduce energy waste, and decrease your utility bills.

Think Small

When you utilize small appliances for small jobs, you save enormous amounts of energy. Reconsider your reliance on that big stovetop and bulky oven by embracing your existing microwave, toaster oven, and pressure cooker instead. Cooking in the microwave reduces cooking energy by as much as 80 percent,[71] while pressure cookers reduce cooking time by about 70 percent. Don't forget the toaster oven, either: if you plan on cooking something small, be sensible by heating the smaller oven.

Be Oven Savvy

Thanks to newer ovens that come to temperature rapidly, preheating is a prehistoric practice. Place foods to be roasted or braised in the oven right away, then turn the oven off five or ten minutes early and let the dishes finish cooking in the oven's residual heat.

Make your oven perform double duty by cooking two items at once. After preparing your protein, place a vegetable in the same pan around the periphery. Doing so saves time, energy, and water—when cleaning up, you will have just one pan to scrub instead of two.

Acquire Stovetop Smarts

Use a properly sized pot for each of the stove burners, as a six-inch pot on an eight-inch electric burner wastes 40 percent of the burner's heat.[72] Use the correct lids atop your pots, too: well-fitted lids keep heat inside and reduce overall cook time. Finally, invest in high-quality cookware with sturdy bottoms, if possible. The ideal pan has a slightly concave bottom, as the metal expands and the bottom flattens out. By contrast, a cheap pan with a warped bottom can use 50 percent more energy to boil water.[73]

Waste Less Water

Most Americans have been fortunate to enjoy clean, running water all their lives. It is no surprise, then, that many overlook this vital resource. But despite easy access from faucets and showers, water is a finite resource that is going extinct.

Even though Earth's natural cycle recycles water, many of our freshwater sources are being drained faster than they are being replenished.[74] Droughts and heatwaves threaten our water supply, as do pollution and fertilizer use, which make existing freshwater unsafe for drinking and irrigation.[75] Worse, thanks to increased population demands, agriculture, and industry construction and manufacturing, the planet's water needs continue to grow. There is a global freshwater crisis, and international cities including Chennai, India, Cape Town, South Africa, and Mexico City stand to face severe water shortages in the coming decades.[76] It is therefore on you and me to waste less water within our homes.

Practical Ways to Conserve Water in the Kitchen

- Repair your dripping faucet.

- Reuse cooking water in the garden. Gardens love pasta and vegetable water, as long as it isn't too salty.

- Use only one drinking glass per person per day.

- Cook with what's leftover in a drinking glass.

- Reuse plates and dishes throughout the day.

- Fill your energy-efficient dishwasher to capacity (and save as much as twenty-four gallons per load as opposed to hand-washing).

- Upgrade your dishwasher to an energy-efficient model if it's more than fifteen years old.

- Use phosphate-free dishwasher detergents that don't pollute waterways.

- Don't pre-rinse dishes before loading the dishwasher

- Drink less coffee and buy fewer avocados and almonds, as these crops are water-intensive.

No Food Waste Here

Reducing food waste requires preparation, organization, and a commitment to using the entirety of a food item (including these carrot fronds, which can be pureed into pesto).

When we waste food, we also waste all the resources that went into growing or raising it, including water and land.

The global food system is responsible for up to one third of all human-caused greenhouse gas emissions, which makes it one of the largest contributors to climate change.[77] And because the United States wastes 40 percent of its food supply,[78] there is huge potential within our own homes to reduce our carbon footprints simply by being more conscious about wasted food.

Meal Plan

Reducing food waste in my own home has been a years-long struggle, and cooking healthy meals for my family once demanded significant mental energy. I dreaded dinner because I never knew what I was serving until the last possible minute. Because weeknights were hectic, I cut corners and resorted to unhealthy and over-packaged convenience meals more often than I preferred. I knew, though, that I could do better with a bit of planning and forethought. Over time, I have come to rely on meal planning to both reduce food waste and ease the daily burden of cooking healthy meals for my family of four.

When done properly, meal planning prioritizes the food items you already have that need to be eaten. The practice saves money, too, because you will not buy more food than you need. If you have never attempted meal planning before and are daunted by the process, know that meal planning is not all that complicated. Indeed, it is simply about planning every meal for the upcoming week and writing out a detailed shopping list before heading to the supermarket. When meal planning for the first time, consider the following three tips:

K.I.S.S.

Keep it simple, silly! Plan easy dinners you know your family will eat. Choose recipes with five ingredients or less whenever possible, as these meals tend to be cheaper, healthier, wrapped in less plastic, and less-time consuming. Embrace the crockpot on busy weekday nights and make one night your leftover night, to ensure you actually eat the entirety of the meals you dutifully plan and prepare.

Use What You Have

Open the refrigerator drawers. Shake the milk carton. Move items around in the pantry. Reacquaint yourself with the freezer, too. Know what you already have before planning a single meal. Doing so will save money and reduce the chances of your food expiring before you consume it.

Embrace Bulk Bin Staples

Supermarket bulk bins overflow with pasta, rice, lentils, and beans. Bring your own containers from home, fill them with items from the bulk bins, and make them the center of your nightly meals. Consider embracing non-meat and non-dairy meals as a sustainable practice—livestock rearing for slaughter contributes to global warming through the methane gas animals produce, as well as to deforestation when acres of trees are cut down to expand pastures.[79] I prefer to make an oversized batch of a single grain at the start of the week and then serve it throughout the week. We'll discuss the ins and outs of bulk bin shopping in the next chapter.

Label and Rotate

Rotating your well-labeled leftovers is a second means of tackling the food waste problem. Label containers with the date you put them into the refrigerator, then rotate them by placing newer leftovers toward the back and pushing older containers forward. To ensure my family remains on board with my labeling efforts, I created an "Eat Me Now" box, a laughably rudimentary (but highly effective!) way to make sure that food nearing expiration gets eaten first. I simply repurposed a child's shoebox and wrote "Eat Me" on it, then put it front and center in the refrigerator. Throughout the week I place foods nearing expiration within it. I've made it a house rule that the contents of the Eat Me Box are eaten first before opening anything new.

Common Concerns and How to Overcome Them

"All those reusable items sound expensive."

Eco-friendly living is often inaccessible to many consumers because of the significant upfront costs associated with investing in reusables. To remedy this, I first suggest letting go of the need to purchase all reusables at once. Second, buy the more expensive items secondhand. Finally, know that you can find most (if not all) reusable items at thrift stores or in your local Buy/Sell/Trade community group.

"Isn't composting time consuming? I'm already stretched thin as it is."

Do you recycle? If so, you likely understand that recycling is not extra work, it's simply different work. The same goes for composting: once you get the hang of it, composting is no more time consuming than recycling, because composting is simply separating a third of your trash.

"There's no way I have the bandwidth to meal plan."

Not long ago, I felt the same way. But although it's counterintuitive, it's true: putting in *more* effort on the front end pays dividends throughout the week. Instead of attempting to plan an entire week's worth of meals, plan and prep just half the dinners for the week instead, then assess whether the nights you planned ran smoothly. If the answer is yes, gradually plan and prep one additional day per week on subsequent planning days. If the answer is no, feel good knowing that you've lost nothing. Go back to what works for you with confidence.

CHAPTER 7

Less Plastic, Please

Have you ever examined the contents of your trash can? If your garbage is like that of most households, it's likely filled with plastic packaging. Nearly 40 percent of the plastic created each year is packaging for single-use products, but very little is recycled.[80]

This staggering statistic is due in part to international exports. In past years, China happily bought America's unwanted paper and plastics. They imported bales upon bales of Americans' recycling; workers then sifted through those bales for items of value that the United States threw away. But the Chinese government restricted this policy in 2017, and as of 2019, they no longer accept America's recyclables.[81]

Unsurprisingly, US municipalities continue to scramble as they come up with feasible disposal options for excess waste. Waste management companies find themselves stuck with recycling that no one wants, and because domestic standards are higher and require more time and labor to sort, they are hit with higher costs associated with processing both trash and recycling. The sad truth is that it's expensive to recycle in America, and some garbage companies quietly cut corners by dumping your recycling in landfills when they think no one is watching.[82]

The Recycling Fallacy

Americans are wild about recycling. Thanks to decades-long efforts urging us to jump on board, most citizens diligently sort their trash from their recyclables before dropping them on the curb each week. You likely assume that your garbage is properly disposed of, and that your recycling *actually* gets recycled. But recycling is overused; worse, it underperforms.

Recycling is a short-sighted Band-Aid to an oversized problem. Recycling programs have tricked us into believing disposability is well-managed by waste treatment facilities. But recycling is a short-sighted Band-Aid to an oversized problem, which, of course, is excessive consumption. In 2017, the most recent year for which national data are available, America generated 267.8 million tons of waste, or approximately 4.5 pounds per person per day.[83]

Have you ever read your municipality's recycling guidelines? If not, you may be recycling unrecyclables, clogging sorting machinery, and ruining entire batches of perfectly good recycling. And because recycling breaks plastic filament chains, the process degrades the material. Recycling plastics is finite: a plastic product can be down-cycled a maximum of ten times on average before becoming garbage.[84]

Plastic and Our Oceans

Over three hundred million tons of plastic are produced every year. Because plastic is lightweight, wind easily carries it from land to river networks. At least thirteen million metric tons of plastic end up in our oceans each year—put another way, a garbage truck's load every minute.[85] Fish, seabirds, turtles, and marine mammals become entangled in bigger debris and ingest smaller pieces. Plastic waste also encourages the growth of pathogens in the ocean, as corals that come into contact with plastic have an 89 percent chance of contracting disease.[86]

It can often feel as though plastic has infiltrated every inch of the planet and, thanks to microplastics research, data prove that it has. Plastic does not simply disappear over time. Instead, it reduces in size into smaller and smaller pieces as it breaks down. A microplastic is a plastic particle less than five millimeters long, and researchers have found microplastics everywhere they look—in our deepest oceans, atop our highest mountains, in the bellies of animals, in rainwater, and in tap water around the world. An Australian study found that humans around the world consume a credit card's worth of plastic each week.[87] And while the sheer prevalence of microplastics is concerning, their lasting effects on our ecosystems are not yet known.

When we examine the scope of the plastics problem and understand fully that plastic has invaded every nook and cranny of our planet, hopelessness is a natural and common response. It may be impossible to completely refuse plastic, but adopting common-sense strategies can significantly reduce the amount of plastic in your home.

Plastic-Free Food Shopping

Reducing plastic starts with intentional food shopping.

When you think about excessive plastic reliance, the first place that probably comes to mind is the grocery store. The first supermarket dates back to 1916. By the 1960s, supermarkets sold 70 percent of the nation's food.[88] Supermarkets capitalize on customers' desire for convenience—instead of running around town to countless stores, you can buy nearly any food and beverage in a single, oversized space. And because the average person grocery shops just one time per week, you likely demand that your food purchases can last without spoilage until at least the following weekend.

But supermarkets have a dirty little secret: they create seemingly endless amounts of plastic garbage in the form of Styrofoam trays, cling wrap, plastic containers, and more. Supermarkets are indeed stores, and stores exist to create a profit. Every damaged or spoiled item is money lost, so supermarkets rely on plastic packaging to preserve their wares.[89]

The most effective way to create less trash is simple: bring home less of it. Here are four ways to reduce your reliance on plastic food and beverage packaging.

1. Expand Your Horizons

Because traditional grocery stores abound with over-packaged food, it's prudent to purchase as much food as possible from places other than the supermarket. Head to your local bakery for fresh bread and put it in a pillowcase to carry it home. Visit the fish market or butcher for your protein, and ask the person behind the counter to pack the items in your lidded glass container.

Local co-ops and health food stores make bulk shopping the center of their business models, and shoppers can therefore fill their own containers with pantry staples like dried beans, lentils, and rice. Remember ethnic grocers, too—many mom-and-pop shops allow customers to fill containers from home. My local Middle Eastern store encourages me to load up on olives, spices, and even cheese in my own jars. You can find stores with bulk bins near you by visiting Zero Waste Home's web-based **BULK app**.

Remember your local produce and dairy farms! My family is fortunate to have an organic farm within miles, and we've invested in the farm's future by signing up for their Community Supported Agriculture (CSA) program. I appreciate that CSA programs provide my family with ultra-fresh vegetables. On many pickup days, farmers have picked our produce just hours before we arrive. I often walk my community's weekly farmer's market, too, because it boasts a wide array of food items from fruits and vegetables, to eggs, meats, and even flowers, all without plastic. Making the farmer's market a weekly excursion enables you to return the containers that delicate foods come in—like berries and cherry tomatoes—on your next visit. And if your family consumes a lot of milk, inquire as to whether you have a local dairy nearby. Many dairy farms recreate a lost era by dropping milk at your doorstep in returnable glass bottles.

2. Use Your Reusable Shopping Kit

Your Reusable Shopping Kit consists of old pillowcases, lidded containers, repurposed jars, and reusable tote bags.

Although I buy nearly all my produce from places other than the supermarket, I still make one trip to a traditional grocery store per week. Before I go, I arm myself with a plan, a list, and my reusable shopping kit.

What's in Your Reusable Shopping Kit?

- 5 old pillowcases. Use one to transport bread from the bakery, and use the others as produce bags for fruits and vegetables.

- 2 large, flat-lidded containers. Ask that your meat and fish selections be packaged in Tupperware instead of disposable paper.

- Several glass jars in various sizes. Place bulk bin items, including rice, grains, oatmeal, popcorn kernels, and more, in jars. Weigh them at home first and write the tare (weight while empty) on a piece of masking tape, then affix it to the bottom of each jar.

- 8 oversized, reusable tote bags. Reusable tote bags are stronger, and therefore more convenient for transporting purchases, than paper or plastic. Fold them neatly, place them and your other shopping kit items in the largest tote bag, and store the entire kit in the trunk of your car, or in a backpack if you rely on public transportation.

The key to creating—and *remembering*—your shopping kit is to repack it as you unpack your groceries. Do not store your purchases in their transport items. Instead, dump your bulk bin rice into its designated kitchen container, then put the jar back in your shopping kit. Place your bread loaf in the bread box or refrigerator before repacking the pillowcase. Finally, make sure to put your whole shopping kit back where it belongs (in my case, my car) immediately after unpacking your groceries. Doing so means you'll be prepared for any spontaneous supermarket trips that may pop up as you go about your errands.

3. Linger among the Produce

Author Michael Pollan argues that eating healthier starts by shopping in the periphery of the supermarket, as produce, meat, and dairy sections line its outer limits. Not surprisingly, these departments also offer food options that are the least processed, salted, and sugared. There's an eco-friendly benefit to hugging the supermarket's periphery, too: doing so means you take home less plastic.

Sustainability at the grocery store ultimately starts by changing your eating habits. A diet that prioritizes local, organic produce and grains is infinitely more eco-friendly than one reliant on processed ones, as excess energy is required to both grind and cook processed foods.[90] And all that plastic packaging? Its manufacturing requires petroleum, and refining petroleum to create plastic pollutes the atmosphere.[91][92]

If the thought of completely changing your diet is daunting, remember that sustainable minimalism advocates for incremental lifestyle tweaks. As you plan your weekly meals, consider making one weeknight dinner meat-free and made from home. Use this weekly opportunity to experiment with plant-based recipes. Reserve ones your family enjoys in a special section of your recipe book, too. Consider embracing meat substitutes like seitan, which boasts both the consistency and chewiness of meat. Over time, expand on your efforts to include a second meat-free meal per week.

Location and Privilege

Low-waste living demands enormous amounts of privilege.

While wealthier citizens don't have to fret about basic necessities like food and shelter, those living in low-income neighborhoods are at a higher risk of being affected by variable resource prices, climate unpredictability, and local environmental degradation.[93] Systemic inequalities exist, and limited access to nutritious foods paired with generalized food insecurity may render eco-conscious purchases impossible for many consumers, especially consumers of color.

Do the best you can with where you are and what's within your budget.

Some areas have more resources than others, and whether or not low-waste living is possible is dependent in part on your geographic location. While urban areas tend to boast bulk and health food stores that allow reusable containers, rural, and even suburban locales offer direct access to farms. If you live in a rural area, inquire as to whether your local farms offer CSA programs. Does your local dairy farm deliver milk the old-fashioned way in glass bottles? Do you have a weekly farmer's market nearby?

Do the best you can with where you are and what's within your budget. If high-quality foods are present in your location but are too expensive, feel good about the changes you *can* make instead of feeling guilty over the ones you can't.

---

4. Be Discerning

Supermarkets present the same product from multiple sellers side by side, so you have the unique opportunity to discern items with eco-friendly packaging from over-packaged items. When presented with a choice between an item in aluminum or the same item packaged in plastic, always choose the former. Similarly, buy items in large quantities, provided you will consume them fully, so as to reduce packages' overall surface area.

Remember, too, that supermarkets exist to make a profit. Samples on toothpicks, buy-one-get-one deals, and weekly circulars are sales tactics that entice you to buy more than you need. The single best strategy for leaving unnecessary plastic at the store is to plan your meals for the week, arm yourself with a detailed shopping list, and when in doubt, simply don't buy.

Real Life Sustainable Minimalists

Organization and Forethought

The younger me never thought much about plastic. But once I did, I noticed it everywhere.

I live in a rural area with few grocery options. While it *is* possible for me to take home less plastic from the supermarket, doing so requires organization and forethought. The good news is that low-waste food shopping gets easier the more I practice.

One of the most impactful ways I reduce my reliance on plastic is by planning meals at home and making a shopping list each week. I make legumes and grains the center of most dinners because I know I can find these items in my supermarket's bulk bins.

When at the grocery store, I almost never take a plastic produce bag. Fruits and vegetables that will be peeled (like bananas, citrus fruits, and cucumbers) go straight into my cart, and other produce items go into one of my reusable produce bags.

At meat and deli counters, I hand over reusable containers. I received many awkward stares and questions at first, and these stares and questions increased my anxiety over being different. But because I tend to shop around the same time each week, the same workers tend to be on shift at that time, so such questions and stares have altogether stopped.

I have made it a house rule that we do not purchase individually wrapped food items. Although this originally felt

impossible as a mother to three children, I was motivated
by the realization that this habit alone has most greatly
reduced the amount of plastic we throw away. The world
may be headed toward single-use disposability, but my
family won't be.

DANIELLA C., podcast listener

Plastic-Free Food Storage

Sustainable minimalists rely on glass, metal, and repurposed waxed cartons to store food.

How did humans survive before Ziplock bags and saran wrap?
The single-use food storage industry may have tricked you into
believing it's impossible to store food—particularly, food you

wish to freeze—without plastic. But the reality is, humans have kept foods in reserve for centuries without it.

Creative food storage practices in your refrigerator, pantry, and freezer both reduce plastic waste and provide non-toxic eating options for your family. Certain chemicals in plastic, including phthalates and BPA, leach out of plastic containers and into food and beverages.[94] And while leached doses are likely low, exposure to low doses over the long term is linked to metabolic disorders, including obesity and reduced fertility. Fatty foods like meats and cheeses are more prone to absorption of such chemicals, and pregnant women and fetuses are at highest risk.[95]

Chemical leaching occurs faster and to a greater degree when a plastic container is exposed to heat. And although some plastic containers are labeled microwave-safe by the US Food and Drug Administration (FDA), researchers recommend erring on the side of caution and avoiding heating foods in plastic containers altogether.[96]

While microwaving accelerates chemical leaching, it can occur even when no microwave is involved. Plastic bottles that hold water and other beverages exhibit leaching when exposed to sunlight.[97] And because the cans that line supermarket shelves are often lined with BPA to prevent corrosion, BPA leaches into food—particularly acidic ones like tomatoes—without any heat whatsoever.[98]

In the Pantry and Refrigerator

My pantry is a beautiful smorgasbord of repurposed jars. The environmentalist in me appreciates that glass is a non-toxic food storage container, and my minimalist side adores the aesthetic that glass jars offer. I keep nearly everything in my pantry, including nuts, lentils, beans, rice, and popcorn kernels, in labeled jars with tight-fitting lids.

Whereas jars similarly extend themselves to refrigerator storage for liquids and semi-liquids, including leftover coffee, extra tomato paste, freshly-squeezed juices, and leftover soups, flat glass or stainless steel containers with lids can also store leftovers with ease. Beeswax wraps are a short-term storage solution for refrigerated items such as cheese, produce, and sandwiches. And for oversized items such as bread, enlist the help of repurposed pillowcases.

No Plastic to See Here

To extend the life of produce without plastic, consider these food-specific tips:

- Lay salad greens on a towel, roll them up, and store them in the crisper.

- Store cabbage, eggplant, and spring onions in the crisper without packaging.

- Place peas and beans on a damp towel, then fold.

- Store artichokes, carrots, and celery in bowls of cold water in the refrigerator.

- Store avocados, strawberries, figs, and berries in a paper bag.

- Store beets, Brussels sprouts, cucumbers, green beans, and radishes in open glass containers covered with a damp towel in the refrigerator.

- Place cauliflower, herbs, and cherries in closed glass containers in the refrigerator.

- Store broccoli rabe, corn, snap peas, spinach, and cut melon in open glass containers in the refrigerator.

In the Freezer

It is entirely possible to freeze food without plastic. Glass jars enable easy freezing of liquid items like soups, sauces, and broths. To prevent glass breakage, reserve an inch of space at the top for contents to expand during freezing. When thawing, place the container directly in the refrigerator to slow the process. Harness the power of glass for freezing food items like casseroles and other pre-made dishes. Containers with tight-fitting lids reduce the chance of freezer burn and enable easy stacking. Stainless steel also freezes exceptionally well, and there's no chance of breakage, either. Opt for bento box-style containers with tight-fitting lids.

While waxed milk, juice, and ice cream cartons are not recyclable in most locations, they offer endless reuse opportunities in the freezer. Because they're waterproof and allow for expansion, waxed cartons work well for freezing soups and sauces. Cut them open at the top, wash them out, and seal with freezer tape.

If you are freezing food for just two to three weeks, wrap the item in unbleached butcher paper, or waxed paper sheets or bags. Double or triple layers for longer freezing periods, and seal any kind of paper wrap with freezer tape.

Packing Lunches without Plastic

Zero-waste lunch boxes feature high-quality gear including a thermos, lidded glass or mental containers, reusable bags, metal silverware, and a cloth napkin.

Citing convenience, many working professionals and school-aged children purchase daily lunches outside the home. And while school meal programs reduce food insecurity for countless children nationwide, making lunches at home reduces the excessive waste that comes along with such pre-packaged options. Although packing homemade lunches can feel tedious, it is absolutely possible to commit yourself to packing plastic-free lunches five days per week.

Homemade lunches demand high-quality, reusable gear, the first of which is a **lunch box**. Choose ones that are well-insulated. For your child, measure it first to ensure it fits easily within their backpack. Velcro tends to lose its efficacy over time and buttons are difficult for little hands to manipulate, so zippered lunch boxes tend to be easiest for lunchers of all ages.

A lunch box's interior benefits from an up-front investment in reusable containers. **Thermoses** encourage food variety by extending homemade lunches beyond ho-hum sandwiches, so make sure you have one for each person in your family. Think beyond the sandwich. Peanut butter and jelly is boring, and thanks to nut allergies, it's prohibited in many schools and workplaces. Twenty-first century lunch boxes are filled with quesadillas, egg croquettes, and vegetable crudités with hummus. Use your thermos to its full potential by packing options like soup with a baguette slice, pasta, oatmeal, and more. Use the thermos to reduce food waste by packing dinner's leftovers for the next day's lunch.

Arm yourself with a set of high-quality, lidded **glass or metal containers**, too, as these are both eco-friendly and non-toxic. Repurpose glass jars you already have. If you're in the market to buy containers, consider purchasing metal over glass, as metal is more school-friendly. Arm yourself with *at least* five glass or metal containers per person, as having extra on hand will enable you to prepare lunches for the entire week at once.

Although Ziplock bags are a common lunch box staple around the world, they are single-use, disposable items. Even if you are committed to reuse, a Ziplock's days are numbered, as they rip in the corners around the lock seal. Many companies sell **reusable bags**, and while some are simply made of sturdier plastic, others are made from silicone, which is preferable. If you're handy with a sewing machine, know that you can easily make them yourself using repurposed fabric. A **beeswax wrap** can be folded into a makeshift bag and works well for this purpose, too.

Finally, no zero-waste lunch box is complete without a **cloth napkin and metal silverware**. Pack a fork and spoon from your kitchen, cut up a piece of old, stained clothing into a square, and finish the edges for an expert DIY cloth napkin.

Helpful Lunch Box Tips

Avoid Experimenting

My earliest attempts at packing lunches invoked creativity, and although I sent unique foods to school with my children, these items almost always returned home uneaten. While I repurposed and reintroduced what I could, I ended up wasting most of these uneaten items. I've since accepted the futility of sending items your child may not eat. Lunch box success is measured by consumption, so stick with your tried and trues. Doing so will reduce both overwhelm and food waste.

Stay Away from Snack Packs

Between extracurriculars, baths, and early bedtimes, weeknights are often hectic. To reduce workweek overwhelm, separate various food items into individual portions on Sunday. I buy crackers and cheese, yogurt, hummus and pita bread, hard-boiled eggs, pickles, olives, and raisins in oversized containers or package-free from bulk bins, and then separate them into small glass containers at home. Because I do all the work on Sunday, I pack an entire week's worth of lunch boxes in under an hour.

Consider buying a bag of pretzels and splitting them into five equal-sized portions, one for each lunch. Better yet, buy corn kernels from the bulk bin and pop enough popcorn to satisfy a week's worth of snacks for the whole family. Mindfully taking the extra step to separate the food into reusable containers pays dividends in both saved money and reduced trash production, while also providing healthier lunch alternatives for your loved ones.

Remember the Food Pyramid

Although the US government replaced the food pyramid with MyPlate in 2011,[99] the original visual designed to help Americans eat balanced meals retains much of its wisdom. A balanced meal is one that is comprised of at least 50 percent fruits and vegetables, with whole grains and varied proteins as well. Dairy should constitute a small portion of your lunch boxes, and sugar should be nearly nonexistent.

Pair the pyramid with common sense as a means of simplifying the lunch packing process. I pack each of my daughters a vegetable or fruit, a protein, a dairy item, and a snack. Nothing more (if I send too much, the healthy stuff comes home uneaten), and nothing less (too little food results in hungry, cranky children by mid-afternoon).

Other Plastic-Free Strategies

Order Takeout Less Often

My family used to order takeout every Friday, and I looked forward to Friday evenings with glee. But takeout creates enormous amounts of single-use waste—main dishes are packaged in lidded plastic, with sauces and accompaniments in smaller, disposable containers. Regularly taking leftovers home after eating at restaurants similarly creates excess waste. Combat this by bringing your own containers from home and using them to transport the uneaten portions of your meal. Similarly, support restaurants that will happily package your takeout order in your glass or steel containers from home when you arrive for pick-up.

Choose the Right Wine

Buy wine in glass bottles instead of boxes lined with plastic. Take pains to buy bottles that utilize natural cork stoppers, too—plastic stoppers contribute to plastic pollution, and metal screw caps contain BPA in the lining. **CORKwatch (recork. com)** lists brands that boast natural cork stoppers over plastic and metal.

Buy Products in Plastic-Free Packaging

Many companies are becoming more conscious about their packaging, and consumers have choices. Some toilet paper brands sell their toilet paper in cardboard boxes without plastic sleeves. The dishwater tablets I purchase (and love) contain no plastic whatsoever, and my laundry detergent comes in a compostable box instead of a plastic jug. When purchasing home products, take the time to research plastic-free options and be sure to read reviews.

Create a Plastic-Free Bathroom

Second to your kitchen, your bathroom likely creates significant plastic waste. Slowly replace single-use disposable items with the following zero-waste reusables:

Reusable Menstrual Products

The average woman uses between 5,000 to 15,000 tampons or pads during her lifetime, a statistic which is entirely preventable.[100] There are countless reusable menstrual products on the market that offer unique solutions, including reusable pads and period underwear (in which the pad is sewn into the underwear). Other options include menstrual cups and discs, which can be worn for up to twelve hours. Sea sponges, too, are hailed by the organic community, and have been used for thousands of years as a zero-waste menstrual product option.

Bamboo Toothbrush

Bamboo toothbrushes are the plastic-free alternative to traditional toothbrushes with nylon bristles. Purchase a bamboo brush with bristles made of boar hair, as these brushes are entirely compostable once it's time to replace them. Alternately, purchase a brush with a bamboo handle and nylon bristles. While not entirely plastic-free, simply snap off the handle to compost it and discard the plastic bristles.

Toothpaste Tablets

Toothpaste tablets are the zero-waste version of traditional, tubed toothpaste. Simply place one on your tongue and get scrubbing.

Handkerchiefs

There's a reason our grandparents embraced handkerchiefs: the reusable solution to runny noses eliminates the need for single-use tissues, for good. My grandmother kept a single handkerchief in each pocketbook so she never found herself without one, and I keep neatly folded stacks in the cupboards of each bathroom for easy access.

Shampoo and Conditioner Bars

Shampoo and conditioner bars are bars of soap for your hair. To help your bars last as long as possible, store them outside of the shower in lidded metal tins.

Coconut Oil

Coconut oil has many beauty care uses. I use coconut oil as my eye makeup remover because I've found that it works better than any commercial product. I also use it as my morning and evening facial moisturizer, as well as in place of body lotion. Relying on a single product for multiple uses eliminates the purchase, and eventual disposal, of several plastic containers.

Reusable Cotton Pads

If you use single-use cotton pads to remove make-up, consider investing in reusable ones. Alternately, make your own by cutting repurposed, 100-percent cotton fabric into a desired diameter and sewing a few pieces together.

Bar Soap

Corporations advertise liquid soap as being more sanitary than bar soap. However, research has debunked this marketing myth.[101] Bar soap is sanitary, plastic-free, and is infinitely cheaper than liquid soap.

Bamboo Cotton Buds

Some brands of cotton swabs, or Q-tips, place cotton on either end of a plastic tube. Forego the plastic variety and purchase ones with a bamboo tube instead. After using, you can compost the entire bud.

Silk Floss

While conventional dental floss is made of wax-covered plastic strands, silk floss provides all the flossing benefits without the disposability—because silk is a natural fiber, you can compost it after flossing.

Safety Razor

Safety razors provide the closest possible shave—even better, they're plastic-free. Opt for a brand that offers a blade take-back program, so that the blade is recycled instead of trashed after it dulls.

Decline Freebies

I used to have the habit of accepting items simply because they were free. Travel-sized shampoo from a hotel? Sure. Pen from the bank? I'll take that, too. I used to believe that if I acquired a needed item for free, I wouldn't have to waste any of my own money. But in reality, I rarely use that travel-sized shampoo and I certainly don't need another pen. Be a ruthless (and plastic-free) gatekeeper. Free items tend to be junk, and allowing them into your home increases the amount of plastic waste you must eventually throw away.

Avoid Microbeads and Glitter

Although microbeads are commonly advertised as essential ingredients in exfoliating personal care products and toothpaste, they're nothing more than tiny pieces of plastic with damaging effects on the environment. Similarly, glitter is a collection of shiny microplastics. Avoid personal care products that contain microbeads, and avoid makeup and art projects with glitter.

Get Cooking

Last year, Ani's school hosted a bake sale fundraiser, and as I perused the table of cookies, cupcakes, and muffins, I noticed that nearly all the food was purchased and woefully over-packaged. Making select food items at home is a powerful way to use less plastic.

An oft-overlooked benefit of cooking at home is healthier eating. By foregoing cellophane-wrapped potato chips and instead making an at-home alternative, you make a healthier version with fewer trans fats and reduced calories. Make a big batch of your favorite snack items, then separate them into silicone bags for easy, single-serve snacking throughout the week. And when you need to grab a snack in a pinch, reach for one of your homemade snack packs.

While zero-waste snacking can be as simple as picking up an apple or cutting up a carrot, the creative possibilities are endless. You can make:

- Kale or cauliflower chips
- Muffins
- Cookies
- Roasted chickpeas
- Hummus, baba ghanoush, and other dips
- Granola bars
- Crockpot yogurt

Consider making your own salad dressings, sauces, and condiments, too, as these items are heavily marked up when purchased at the supermarket. Dressings and sauces last a long time in the refrigerator, so making them at home will save money and reduce packaging waste.

Common Concerns and How to Overcome Them

"My kids are picky eaters. I doubt they'd snack on healthy foods."

Virtually every food can be separated at home, including your children's favorites. First identify their favorite snack items, then decide how you can make a lower-waste option. Do they like cheese? If so, buy a big slab of cheese and cut it yourself into individual portions. What about yogurt? Buy the biggest container the supermarket sells, then divvy it up. Potato chips? Less-healthy foods also benefit from being divided at home: simply buy a big bag and place them in single-portion reusable ones.

"Is plastic packaging the only consideration newbies should make when being more eco-friendly?"

While it is certainly important to consider packaging waste when purchasing food, it is also prudent to consider where and how an item was produced. Buying local food whenever possible reduces carbon emissions associated with transport over long distances, and strengthens local economies by supporting nearby farms. Similarly, organic food by definition is grown without planet-polluting chemicals. Try to purchase local, organic produce in minimal packaging whenever possible by asking if there's a weekly local farmer's market near you. Alternately, consider investing in your local vegetable farm by signing up for a seasonal CSA program.

"My daughter suffers from celiac disease and I'm concerned that bulk bins are contaminated with items made with gluten. What do I do?"

Many supermarkets offer gluten-free alternatives, but they are almost always wrapped in excessive plastic. And while some bulk bins offer a drop-down option (meaning no scoop is needed), there's no way to know whether the bin once held an item with gluten. If you'd like to live plastic-free but are concerned about cross-contamination, emphasize package-free starchy items like potatoes, yams, and squash. Buy nuts from your local farmer's market, too, where there is no danger of residual gluten. Alternately, buy gluten-free foods like millet, quinoa, and others in the largest packages you can find. Because there's less packaging per surface area, buying big bags reduces the total amount of packaging.

CHAPTER 8

Carbon Footprints and On-the-Go Sustainability

The Refuse the Straw campaign highlighted a grim reality: each day, Americans collectively discard 500 million straws. Due to consumer pushback, Seattle became the largest US city to ban plastic straws in July 2018. Starbucks, Alaska Airlines, and other corporations also responded to public outcry with programs to phase out straws and stirrers.[102]

But although the anti-straw movement spotlighted America's over-reliance on single-use straws, the movement failed to extend itself to other plastics that are used and then tossed when on-the-go. Refusing straws and recycling are weakened by an identical Achilles heel: both seemingly eco-friendly behaviors are in many ways environmentally detrimental because they give consumers a false sense of efficacy. And because many assume that just refusing a straw at a restaurant has an oversized impact, they neglect to do more.

While reducing your reliance on plastic is an important aspect of sustainability, reducing your carbon footprint is tantamount.

What's a Carbon Footprint?

Greenhouse gases trap heat in our atmosphere and warm the planet, and a warming planet contributes to climate change. Climate change is responsible for a host of environmental problems, including melting glaciers, sea level rise, and increased intensity and frequency of severe weather patterns like hurricanes, heat waves, wildfires, and droughts.[103] There are physical, biological, and psychological consequences to climate change, too. Public health officials argue that premature deaths due to severe weather phenomena, changes in food distribution, and increased water-borne illnesses threaten the human race.[104]

Many daily activities—using electricity, driving a car, heating your home, and making purchases—emit greenhouse gases into the atmosphere. But exactly how many greenhouse gases do your unique daily behaviors generate? Enter carbon footprints.

Your carbon footprint is the total amount of greenhouse gases generated by your daily actions and is commonly measured in metric tons. You can calculate your unique carbon footprint at www.nature.org.

The average carbon footprint for a person living in the United States is a whopping 16 metric tons, one of the highest rates in the world.[105] The worldwide per person average is closer to 4 tons.[106] Yet the Intergovernmental Panel on Climate Change (IPCC) warns that it is imperative to prevent a warming of more than 1.5 degrees Celsius (about 34.7 degrees Fahrenheit) by

2050.[107] To achieve this, every human on earth must reduce their carbon footprints to just 2 metric tons per year.

While lifestyle habits within the home—including what you eat and how many children you choose to have—increase or decrease your unique carbon footprint, intentional choices outside the home can substantially reduce your impact.

The Five Tenets of Carbon Footprint Reduction

1. Drive Less (or Not at All)

Public transportation reduces air pollution, saves money, and is up to ten times safer than commuting by automobile.[108]

Daily transportation habits greatly influence your carbon footprint, and living without a car conserves about 2.6 tons of CO_2 annually.[109] Driving less, walking, biking, and taking public transit are common-sense ways to decrease your reliance on automobiles for travel.

If living without a car is impractical, take pains to reduce emissions whenever possible. First, invest in a hybrid or electric car, if doing so is financially feasible. Because hybrids run on both an internal combustion engine and an electric motor, they require less fuel and therefore lower greenhouse gases emissions by as much as 46 percent.[110] And electric cars, while not necessarily zero-carbon, boast zero tailpipe emissions.[111]

When driving, go easy on the gas and breaks. Make sure your tires are properly inflated, as low tire pressure will hurt your fuel economy. Use the car's air conditioning less and cruise control more.[112] Finally, batch your errands and plan your route in a logical manner before leaving the house, as doing all your errands in a single trip reduces unnecessary emissions.

Real Life Sustainable Minimalists

Intentional Automobile Use

I've implemented three key steps into my daily life to reduce reliance on my car. First, I found a sustainable company to deliver toilet paper, dish, and laundry pods right to my door. Second, I meal plan, so I only drive to the grocery store once a week. Finally, I batch and plan my family's errands so that I either do them all in a single trip or have my husband stop on his way home from work as he passes the stores.

LAUREN W., Sustainable Minimalists group member

2. Travel Smart

Passenger airplanes emit significant amounts of greenhouses gases into the atmosphere, and a single round-trip flight from New York to Europe creates a warming effect equivalent to two to three tons of carbon dioxide per person.[113] Although flying less (or not at all) substantially reduces your impact on the planet, many minimalists value vacations for their emphasis on moments of quality instead of trinkets of quantity. And while vacations create lasting memories with your family, traveling has a bad reputation as being decidedly eco-unfriendly.

The good news is that sustainable travel is not a passing trend, but a lifestyle choice that creates a positive effect on communities visited. Enacting practical measures on your next vacation can ensure you enjoy your holiday without harming the planet.

Planning Your Trip

The only way to make air travel sustainable is to avoid it.

The most impactful eco-travel decisions happen at home. As you plan your trip, choose a destination that doesn't require air travel, as the only way to make air travel sustainable is to avoid it. Consider traveling to your desired destination by train or another means of public transit that seats at least forty people. Alternately, seek out hidden gems in your area: doing so means you'll spend less time traveling and more time vacationing.

If you must fly, fly smart. Business class, with its extra legroom and bigger seats, emits approximately three times more emissions than coach. Offset your carbon footprint by flying coach, and fly direct instead of choosing an itinerary with layovers that have excessive gas-guzzling takeoffs and landings.

Before booking your lodging, seek out and support sustainable accommodations. Support a holistically sustainable hotel, lodge, or bed & breakfast that supports environmental, social, and economic issues. Such lodging will use renewable energy, conserve water, employ effective waste reduction measures, and give back to their local communities. Consider staying at an Airbnb—having a kitchen will enable you to cook more and waste less.

Packing for Your Trip

Oversized suitcases hold us back and slow us down. Embrace a smaller suitcase instead and just pack the essentials. Bring comfortable, versatile shoes you can walk long distances in, and pack multi-purpose items that dry quickly. A sarong can transform itself into a blanket, a towel, a scarf, a pillow, or a dress, and a one-piece bathing suit can double as a shirt with pants over it.

Packing your own personal care products will empower you to decline free travel-sized shampoos, conditioners, and lotions, all of which are packaged in miniature plastic bottles. Create your own plastic-free travel set with a bamboo toothbrush, dental tablets, silk floss, shampoo, conditioner, and any other items you'll need while on vacation. Don't be afraid to transfer your toiletries into smaller, TSA-approved containers as a means of ensuring your liquids do not get confiscated at the airport's security checkpoint.

Don't forget the reef-safe sunscreen, either! While conventional sunscreens contain toxic ingredients that harm ocean ecosystems and kill coral reefs, "reef-safe" varieties are made with minerals like zinc oxide or titanium oxide (however, you should do your research to validate products with "reef-safe" claims).[114]

If traveling by air, eliminate the need for single-use disposables on your flight. Bring your own water bottle and fill it once you're through the security checkpoint. If you're flying internationally, call your airline ahead of time to refuse the cellophane-wrapped meal. Bring snacks and sandwiches as a means of avoiding snacks packaged in plastic. Finally, refuse the airline's headphones by packing your own.

On Vacation

As you vacation, anchor your actions to a singular goal: leave your destination better than you found it. Because not all countries have comprehensive systems for managing waste in place—some developing countries may not have waste management systems at all—it is therefore prudent to commit to creating as little waste as possible when on vacation. Download city maps, local transportation apps, and travel guides directly to your phone as a means of creating less waste. Skip single-use plastics like utensils and cups on your travels by carrying reusables with you. Head to a nearby grocery store and stock up on healthy snacks that are produced with less packaging. You may not be able to avoid plastic entirely, but you can certainly avoid the mini bar's single-serving sizes, all of which are overpriced and overpackaged.

Being judicious with your giving—and with your dollars—can go a long way in developing destinations.

Seek out local, hand-crafted items instead of mass-produced souvenirs as a means of ensuring that your money is channeled back into the community. Buffets result in mounds of uneaten food, so decline meals at your hotel's. Instead, support local business owners by visiting restaurants off the beaten track and ordering food that's in season for the location.

Finally, be conscious of your energy use by enacting common-sense measures. Walk, cycle, or use public transportation as much as possible. Turn off lights, reuse towels, and decline housekeeping, too.

3. Create Less Trash

Recycling according to your municipality's guidelines can lower your carbon footprint.[115] And while reducing the amount of waste your home produces by reducing, reusing, and recycling is a prudent first step, it is also both important (and entirely possible!) to reduce the amount of waste you produce when on-the-go.

On-the-Go Essentials

As you go about your day, keep essential reusables with you, including handkerchiefs, reusable water bottles, a coffee mug, a bento box, silverware wrapped in a cloth napkin, and more.

The best way to reduce waste when outside the home is to make certain you have everything you may need on hand. Rather than going through multiple single-use tissues, keep four handkerchiefs with you at all times in a pouch in your handbag. Let the pouch double as transport for soiled handkerchiefs.

Coca-Cola produces 3,400 plastic water bottles every second, each of which is destined to become waste.[116] Instead of contributing to the problem, keep one **water bottle** on hand per person to ensure you won't resort to buying plastic ones when you're on-the-go. Heading to a restaurant with your children? Bring water bottles for them as a means of declining those disposable, lidded cups and straws.

Because plastic lines paper cups and Styrofoam is very difficult to recycle, most disposable coffee cups become trash shortly after your beverage is finished. If you're in the habit of purchasing coffee outside the home, hand your **reusable mug** to the barista instead of taking your coffee to go in a single-use, disposable one.

Avoid purchasing snacks in plastic packaging by **packing snacks at home**. Use the same strategies you use when packing zero-waste lunches: buy in bulk when possible, make many at once, then separate them into snack-sized portions. If you don't have the time to prepare snacks in advance, grab a food item that's wrapped in natural packaging. Some fruits, like bananas and citrus varieties, boast skin that acts as nature's packaging. If you're taking along a different fruit, such as an apple, peach, or pear, rinse it and wrap it in a tea towel. The towel performs double duty as both waste-free packaging and as a napkin. Alternately, take along a hard-boiled egg. Its shell is its packaging, not plastic.

A **bento box** is a reusable, Japanese-style lunch box with three lidded containers of various sizes, each of which fits nicely within the other. Store a lightweight bento box in your handbag as a means of declining plastic containers from restaurants. If you go out to eat and have leftovers to take home, simply package them in your bento box. Similarly, utilize bento boxes to take compostable materials home instead of trashing them. If you bring a banana to the playground, for example, pack the peel back up in your bento box and compost it once you return home.

In an effort to waste fewer plastic utensils and napkins, create a **silverware wrap** for every person in your household by wrapping a fork, knife, and spoon in a **cloth napkin** and securing the bundle with a repurposed bread tie. If you don't own extra silverware, purchase camping silverware, as it is lightweight and will likely fold.

If you rely on your car as your main mode of transportation, keep your **Reusable Shopping Kit** in your trunk. Doing so will grant you the preparedness you need for sustainability outside of the home without the hassle of carrying bulky reusables in your handbag. (If, however, you rely less on your car for transportation, store your kit in a backpack for easy transport.) Use certain parts of your kit during various errands beyond the supermarket. Making a quick stop to the pharmacy? Bring a reusable tote in with you to decline their plastic bags. Grabbing a slice of pizza from your neighborhood pizzeria? Hand over a glass Tupperware from your shopping kit for guilt-free transport.

Real Life Sustainable Minimalists

On Being OK with Being Silly

My sustainable choices sometimes look silly, and I'm OK with it. Here's an example: Sometimes, I put my fruits and vegetables straight into my cart. I'd rather buy them loose than use a plastic bag, and I'll wash them once I get home anyway. This quirky habit often strikes up conversations with others, and it's always a joy to share my sustainability practices.

Another way I'm happily silly is by vetting restaurants. Enjoying meals out of the house is one of my favorite hobbies, and I choose to frequent restaurants that offer a variety of plant-based options and use minimal plastic. I ask myself and my dining partners silly questions before visiting: Does the restaurant ask if patrons want straws, or is it their practice to simply place them on the table? If a condiment is requested, does the server put it in a small, reusable container or a one-time-use plastic container? When ordering online, is there a "no cutlery needed" option? These details may seem insignificant, but these types of behaviors speak to whether a restaurant has sustainability in mind.

DANIELLE STEINBOCK, Sustainable Minimalists group member

4. Shop Less

Because most products require nonrenewable resources to get produced—and because crude oil is relied upon to manufacture the packaging used to ship them—purchasing unneeded items steals from the planet. One of the best ways we can protect earth's nonrenewable resources and prevent unnecessary greenhouse gases from entering the atmosphere is to buy fewer commercial products.

Online Versus In-Store

If you're wondering whether there's an eco-friendly way to shop, the short answer is no.

If you're like the average consumer, you likely buy many items from the convenience of your home. Yet you do not purchase *everything* online, and thus rely on other modes of transportation—most notably your automobile—to conduct errands. The result is excessive carbon emissions from delivery trucks, freight airplanes, and cars.

The US annually ships 165 billion packages, wasting approximately one billion trees' worth of cardboard.[117] There are emissions considerations associated with the shipments of all those packages, too: delivery companies invest significant time and resources determining efficient delivery routes, but online shopping has not reduced the amount of cars on the road. And even though consumers are purchasing more and more online,[118] there's an overall increase in travel time, traffic delays, and vehicle emissions on many US roads and highways.

Online shopping with intention can be more eco-friendly than shopping at brick-and-mortar stores. Purchase all the items you need online when possible to reduce emissions associated with driving your car to a store. Decline speedy shipping by always opting for ground delivery, and fill your shopping cart over the course of an entire week. By batching your items into a single purchase you'll likely reduce both the packaging waste and the need for multiple delivery trucks to stop at your home.

5. Consider Carbon Offsets

After you've taken conscious steps to reduce your carbon footprint, purchase carbon offsets to neutralize your environmental impact.

Purchasing carbon offsets compensates for your emissions by helping to fund a carbon-reducing project that plants trees, builds wind farms, conserves forests, or invests in other forms of renewable energy. **Carbonfund.org** lists practical donation guidelines for consumers who wish to offset their impact.

Other Ways to Practice On-the-Go Sustainability

Dry Clean Less

A French factory worker's maid first invented dry cleaning by accident in the nineteenth century after she spilled lamp oil on a soiled tablecloth. When the tablecloth dried, the soiled areas had all but disappeared.[119]

Dry cleaning is the process of cleaning garments in a liquid other than water, and while the first dry cleaners relied on flammable solvents like kerosene and gasoline, the industry has since evolved. Up to 90 percent of dry cleaners in the United States now use the colorless hydrocarbon perchloroethylene (PERC) to clean delicate garments.

Yet dry cleaning continues to pose an environmental threat due to pollution emitted by the process. PERC released during the dry cleaning process lingers for decades as an air pollutant, and it contaminates water and soil when dry cleaners improperly dispose of it.

Dry cleaning also poses significant health concerns. PERC is a suspected human carcinogen that enters the human body through both inhalation and skin exposure. It is linked to cancer, liver disease, kidney disease, and reproductive disorders.[120] And because PERC is absorbed through skin exposure, the full effects on consumers who clothe themselves in garments recently cleaned with PERC remain unknown.

Wet cleaning stands in stark contrast to dry cleaning and is considered an environmentally-sensitive cleaning method.[121] Because wet cleaning uses water and detergent, the process eliminates air and water pollution, as well as the detrimental health effects associated with PERC.[122] Inquire as to whether you have a wet cleaner in your community, and if so, frequent it.

If you do frequent a wet or dry cleaner, be sure to return the cleaner's metal hangers. Ask, too, that it is written in your preferences to not wrap your clothes in plastic bags.

Spearhead Green Teams

The average American professional works 8.8 hours a day, or 44 hours per week, outside the home.[123] And American children? Children who attend public school spend 6.6 hours per day within a schoolhouse's walls.[124] Because the majority of Americans' weeks are spent at work and school, both spaces have the potential to transform themselves from waste-producing powerhouses into collaborative hubs that educate on the importance of incremental sustainability.

Both schools and offices benefit from common-sense measures, including limiting paper use (or going paperless entirely) and turning off technology like computers, printers, copiers and scanners at the end of each day. If you traditionally commute to work or drop your child off at school in your automobile, working even just one day per week from home and signing your child up for school bus pickup will significantly reduce your carbon footprint. An even greater reduction would occur by forgoing scheduled business trips that require air travel and hosting virtual meetings instead.

If you work in an office, you have a unique opportunity to create lasting change by spearheading a Green Team. Green teams invite others to brainstorm and subsequently implement eco-friendly initiatives at their place of employment. Some smart initiatives to implement are:

- Shifting as many business purchases as possible to local vendors. Doing so will restrict purchases from traveling long distances on diesel-burning trucks, as well as support your local economy.

- Replacing disposable products in the staff kitchen with reusable ones. Be sure to also provide dish soap for employees to wash what they use.

- Taking existing trash reduction efforts one step further by enacting a composting system.

- Adding greenery. Plants purify air by removing toxins.

Common Concerns and How to Overcome Them

"I'd like to be more sustainable outside of the home, but it sounds like so much work."

Although reducing your carbon footprint on excursions will feel like extra work in the beginning, as with all new habits, it will get easier. While it takes just two or three days to foster a bad habit, it takes sixty-six days on average to create a positive one.[125] Give yourself at least two months to tweak your efforts, then watch them stick.

"I hate being judged, and I often find it's easier to just blend in."

Although I am extroverted by nature, I, too, felt nervous the first time I handed over my glass Tupperware at a restaurant and my reusable mug at a coffee shop. Even though standing out goes against your nature, I urge you to attempt eco-friendly behaviors anyway. Commit to going out of your comfort zone ten times, because each time you practice on-the-go sustainability will feel easier than the last.

"I love traveling the world and visiting famous sites and cities. Are you saying I can't travel anymore?"

I love traveling too, and my husband and I did a lot of it before having children. Consider visiting local, less-traveled locales as opposed to high-trafficked ones, and reconsider your desire to visit endangered sites. Travelers who want to "see a place before it's gone" often do more harm to the habitat than good, as more foot traffic results in further degradation of the endangered area. Similarly, embrace incrementalism. If the thought of never traveling again leaves a bad taste in your mouth, consider traveling *less* as a practical first step toward sustainability.

CHAPTER 9
Gifting and Thrifting

Embracing secondhand saves money, encourages responsible decluttering, and prevents additional items from entering the waste stream.

When I was a child, my mother occasionally rented a table at a gigantic flea market in a neighboring town. We would gather our unwanted items in oversized boxes, schlep them to the market, and attempt to make some sales. As my mother manned the booth, my grandmother, sister, and I would roam the crisscrossing pathways lined with other people's junk. It was cluttered, cavernous chaos in which the adults seemed to be having an awful lot of fun. As an adult, I, too, have learned that there is something thrilling about finding that diamond in the rough that's being sold for a fraction of its actual value.

I embraced thrifting secondhand items shortly after Lara was born. By then I had learned that kids don't care about wearing name-brand clothes—they either grow out of them too fast, or stain and ruin them at first wear. She had all her sister's hand-me-downs anyway, but on the rare occasion Lara needed an item, I asked around in my community first. My neighbors generously passed along their no-longer-needed bibs, snow suits, toys, and more. On the even rarer occasion that I needed to buy her something, I bought it secondhand.

I've since expanded my thrifting efforts beyond kids' clothes and into parts of my home. My family's home has a porch that overlooks our backyard. It really is quite a serene space, but it's enclosed only by screens, so while the space is lovely in late spring and summer, chilly autumns and long winters render it useless for more than half the year. Because it's just a two-season room, I saw no sense in buying new furniture for it. I am still surprised at how easy—and how fun!—it was to acquire a secondhand outdoor table that seats four. I decorated the space by "shopping" my own home for items we already owned, including a mirror for the side wall and two lanterns for atop the table. Haig smartly strung a string of lights on one of the beams, and suddenly the room felt complete. We completely furnished our sunroom for under $100.

The Gift Economy, Explained

We live in a society that reveres the latest and greatest, not the old and weathered. While many financially unstable consumers rely on thrifting as less of a lifestyle choice and more of a necessity, disposable incomes make shiny, new goods accessible to the middle and upper classes. Yet trinkets with stories infuse homes with character, and one-of-a-kind garments impart playfulness on otherwise pedestrian wardrobes.

Imagine a world in which you buy very, very little. This world already exists, and its wonder comes in the form of the gift economy.

Gifting has been around for centuries, and such economies rely on relationships, not personal gain, to spread love and share resources. While market economies tend to be quite impersonal, gift economies encourage reciprocal giving to both foster social bonds and strengthen community resilience.

Gifting is a joyous way to be eco-friendly. Regular participants of local gift economies report that gifting is a joyous way to be eco-friendly. The benefits of gifting on the giver are well-documented, and gifting to neighbors is similar to participating in volunteer service—both habits give back to the community in which you live.

While gifting is indeed different than thrifting—the latter generally involves a monetary transaction—cultivating a thrifting habit prevents new items from entering the waste stream while also sending corporations the message that you're uninterested in seeing additional goods enter the market. Embracing gifting and thrifting economies is as easy as harnessing the power of the internet and scoring great secondhand deals from the comfort of your own home.

Thrifting and Gifting's Benefits

Beyond eco-friendliness, thrifters and gifters report other benefits to these practices , including:

Saves Money

Although minimalists revere quality over quantity, quality items are often expensive. In instances where new, well-made items are financially inaccessible, thrifting and gifting make quality purchases possible at a fraction of the price.

Consider furniture: it has never been easier to purchase trendy and cheap pieces of furniture, but such items break, buckle, scratch, and lose their overall appeal within a decade. When I found myself on the hunt for a new desk, I knew I wanted a solidly constructed desk made of real wood, not particleboard. I wanted it to command attention in my office, and I wanted it to be heavy with drawers that refused to buckle under a bit of weight.

Although new desks like the one I described are expensive, secondhand ones are more financially palatable. To meet my contemporary taste, I purchased a vintage writing desk refurbished by a local craftsman for a fourth of the going rate of a new, quality one.

Antique furniture is often given away in gifting groups. Because antiques are of high-quality by definition, embracing secondhand enables you to own well-crafted pieces with decades of life still left to give.

Encourages Responsible Decluttering

Although removing without tossing is a pillar of sustainable decluttering, finding homes for your no-longer-loved possessions can be both time consuming and inconvenient. Gifting is the easiest and quickest way to responsibly declutter, and the process is as simple as snapping photos of your unwanted possessions and uploading them to your local gifting platform. While selling your items will likely entail a bit more work, you can rest easy knowing you sold your items to people who genuinely want and need them.

Appreciates Uniqueness

Thanks to their pages upon pages of glossy, minimalist inspiration, home decor catalogs speak to consumers that are fed up with clutter. It used to be that I would leaf through *Crate & Barrel*, *Pottery Barn*, or some other home decor catalog because I desired the perfect *thing* to transform my home from a messy, lived-in disaster to a pristine one with clean lines, white furniture, and nary a whiff of clutter. It took me a long time to realize, however, that home decor catalogs overlook something vital: they intentionally leave absent all the items that make a house a home.

Inserting thrifted and gifted pieces into your decor infuses the attributes catalogs lack, including character, craftsmanship, and a real-life, lived-in quality. It invites a sense of history, too, especially if you invite family heirlooms into the mix. To create a space that is visually entertaining, consider adding select and unexpected trinkets with stories to your decor.

Supports Others

Instead of buying from a chain store in which your money directly increases the wealth of already-wealthy executive boards, buying secondhand from national organizations like Goodwill and The Salvation Army is a donation to charity, and the proceeds from your sale support families in need.

Thrifting for clothes and accessories prioritizes workers' rights within the fashion industry, too. Sweatshop garment workers around the world labor for eighteen-hour days, seven days per week during peak season, and rarely earn more than two dollars per day.[126] Thrifting is a tangible way for consumers to take a stand against modern-day slavery because doing so drives down consumer demand for cheap sweatshop goods.

Real Life Sustainable Minimalists

A Game of Hide and Seek

When I moved into my own apartment for the very first time, I owned nothing except a bed and a dresser; I didn't even own a fork. I had nothing, so I had to find a way to find everything I needed to furnish my new home.

While I once would have gone to stores like Ikea and HomeGoods to get what I needed, I instead browsed secondhand marketplaces and thrifted every single item for my new apartment. In the end, I furnished the entire space—from the furniture to the forks—for under $500.

For me, thrifting is really just a game of hide and seek. I get to talk to different people and peek into their lives and homes. The process has fostered connections to my furniture, as they have stories that add to the character of my home. It's nice to come back to a space that is filled with things I picked out and love.

AMANDA L., episode #033 podcast guest

Common Misconceptions

I once harbored antiquated notions of both gifting and thrifting. Admittedly, I envisioned moth-ball-smelling clothes, broken appliances, and an awful lot of junk.

I'm not alone. I polled members in The Sustainable Minimalists Facebook group to gauge their greatest thrifting concerns, and they overwhelmingly reported reluctance over the practice because they perceive these items to be old and used. And yes, while secondhand items are often used, the reality is they weren't used all that much. Americans live in an increasingly disposable society in which we use nearly everything we own just a handful of times before discarding them for newer versions. Once you begin thrifting, you will likely have a shocking realization: because secondhand items are often in great condition, they are likely indistinguishable from new versions. Indeed, thrifting makes incredible opportunities possible for consumers who are willing to forego the notion that new is best.

Members in our Facebook group also reported that their ambivalence to thrifting is due to the assumption that secondhand purchases are dirty. If an item is old and used, isn't it also unsanitary? Yet washing before using is standard practice for both new and secondhand purchases. After buying a set of brand-new mugs, you likely wash them before storing them in the cabinet. You likely toss brand-new clothes in the washing machine, too, before wearing them for the first time. Inspect thrifted items before purchasing, then clean and disinfect them at home, just as you would if the items were brand new.

A final barrier members reported is a lack of interest in rummaging around unorganized thrift stores to spot a good deal. While thrifting once meant sifting through piles at yard sales and flea markets in the hopes of finding a treasure, the internet has revolutionized the secondhand shopping game. If you've never thrifted before and don't know where to start, I suggest starting on the World Wide Web.

Where to Gift

Giving and accepting items for free within your community negates the need for shipment of goods across far distances. The local options I've listed below harness the power of community while eliminating unnecessary carbon emissions related to shipment.

Buy Nothing Project

The Buy Nothing Project describes itself as a "worldwide social movement" with community groups in over thirty countries. The movement advocates for gifting time, gratitude, help, and physical possessions as a means of bringing people together. Joining your local group is as easy as searching for your location at **buynothingproject.org**. Be on the lookout for items others are giving away. Alternately, strengthen your gift economy as you sustainably declutter by offering your unwanted items to others.

Real Life Sustainable Minimalists

Why Gifting Works

The Buy Nothing Project has transformed my world. I have been able to give away so much when purging our space and I've received items with intention to maximize our increasingly sustainable lifestyle. Clothes, kids toys, cleaning stuff, tools—*anything* comes and goes! Toilet paper cardboard rolls for school projects! Egg cartons! It's a beautiful thing when done right. The Buy Nothing Project has enriched my local mama tribe immensely.

PAIGE K., podcast listener

Facebook

Aptly named Curb Alert, my little New England town has a very active Facebook group for secondhand steals. The premise is simple: give away your unwanted items to others nearby for free. Simply stick the item on your curb, take a picture of it, and post your address in the closed Facebook group. The first person to pick up the item keeps it.

While I have received countless gems through Curb Alert, including a working deep freezer, children's clothes, and dozens of toys, my greatest joy is the way the group enables me to easily and quickly declutter. The group's rules ask that you simply place no-longer-needed items on your curb–there's no longer a need to store things until you find time to bring them to a donation center. Inquire as to whether your community has a similar Facebook group. If not, consider creating one yourself.

Where to Thrift

eBay

Many international internet platforms both facilitate the secondhand shopping process and expand the scope of a thrifter's hunt. The oldest and probably the most well-known thrifting website is **eBay**. There are opportunities for those on both sides of the buying and selling transaction, and while the seller pays the site a portion of their earnings, the buyer traditionally pays for shipping.

Etsy

Although **Etsy** is best known for its adorable assortment
of handcrafted jewelry and homemade beauty products, it
can also be a secondhand shopper's dream marketplace.
Secondhand clothing, refurbished furniture, and upcycled
goods with artistic flair are all fair game on Etsy. Thanks to the
site's emphasis on reviews from real buyers, I felt confident
purchasing a refurbished coffee table on Etsy, and I still adore
it nearly a decade later.

Facebook Marketplace

Facebook Marketplace encourages secondhand shopping
and is increasing in popularity because it ameliorates safety
concerns associated with anonymous buy-sell transactions.
Use Facebook Marketplace to sell items within your own
community. If you're on the hunt for something specific, use
Marketplace's search bar and refine your search by entering
your zip code.

Poshmark

From fast fashion to high fashion, **Poshmark** offers items
from over five thousand clothing brands. Its smartphone app
enables buyers to filter products based on size, color, brand,
and more, and you can filter results based on brands you love
that are "New with Tags." You may appreciate the site's offer/
counter-offer feature that encourages bargaining, and when
you need to purchase many items, you can bundle purchases
from the same seller for extra savings.

ThredUp

ThredUp does all the hard work of selling your clothing and accessories for you, including inspecting, photographing, writing detailed descriptions, and shipping. They also take care of the payment and send you your portion of earnings when an item sells. The process is as easy as ordering ThredUp's Clean Out Kit and filling it with your unwanted items. For the clothes that do not sell, ThredUP responsibly recycles them. You can buy on ThredUp, too, with significant ease.

Worn Wear

Worn Wear is an online thrift shop that exclusively sells Patagonia products and makes them more financially accessible to consumers of all income levels. Worn Wear maintains a high level of quality control and repairs items that are ripped or torn in-house before selling them on the site.

Tradesy

Tradesy specializes in high-end, designer clothing brands for women. And while items listed on the site are more expensive than those on Poshmark or ThredUp, Tradesy is the place to find great steals on expensive garments. The site offers a 100-percent authenticity promise, ensuring that you are not buying a knockoff. You may find that you agree with Tradesy's mission, which advocates for simplifying wardrobes and paying a bit more for quality items that can be treasured for years and years.

Refashioner

It can be difficult—if not downright impossible—to find vintage clothing on sites like Poshmark and ThredUp. Enter **Refashioner**, which makes finding high-quality vintage items from the 1920s and onward possible. The company boasts meticulous quality control, and I appreciate that many of their pieces come with a story, too.

Neo Thread Co.

Neo Thread Co. believes that there's beauty to be found in discarded clothes. Their designers transform hum-drum, secondhand items into fresh garments while also committing to using recyclable packaging materials.

Helpful Tricks

...because e-commerce breaks down barriers to buying, it is your responsibility to build those barriers back up.

I made some regrettable purchases in my early days as a young thrifter. I found myself completely swept away by a knee-length, 100-percent wool cardigan from a reputable brand with tags on my first visit to Poshmark. I purchased it quickly—too quickly, if I'm being honest— before anyone else perusing the site had a chance to snag the deal. I neglected to practice intentionality, ignoring the fact that the cardigan was a want and not a need. These days, that wool cardigan sits in my closet, largely unworn.

Although the hunt for inexpensive, quality finds can quickly become addicting, the rules of conscious consumerism *always* apply. Because cost savings from shopping secondhand can be enormous, it may be the case that you find yourself purchasing more than you need. But accepting an excess of *anything*—whether gifted, thrifted, or new—creates clutter in the home you aspire to keep tidy. Remind yourself that because e-commerce breaks down barriers to buying, it is your responsibility to build those barriers back up. Does the item you are spying speak to your authentic self? What are the hidden costs associated with the purchase that you may be forgetting?

If you plan to visit a brick-and-mortar thrift store, know that weekends are busiest. Lessen overwhelm by going during the week when crowd size is reduced. Arm yourself with a list and measuring tape, and commit to being both choosy and patient. If you don't find the item you were looking for, refuse to settle for an item that is less than ideal. Remember that inventory changes by the hour, so commit to trying again another day.

If you're in the market for an appliance or an electronic, test the item before you buy it. Make sure it has all its parts, too, including a power cord if the item requires one. If you're considering a piece of furniture, be sure to measure it first so you're certain it will fit in the space you want to put it.

In the cases of health and safety, it may be smarter to buy a new model than an out-of-date, potentially defective secondhand version. It's impossible for potential thrifters to know the full picture of an item's life before it was donated; as such, I suggest that you not thrift safety items, including bike helmets and car seats. Once a helmet is involved in an accident, its ability to protect the head from future collisions is reduced. The case is similar with children's car seats—current regulations recommend disposing of any car seat that has been involved in a crash. Secondhand mattresses, although not a safety item, can likewise pose health risks. Mattresses house bed bugs that lay their eggs in the crevices. Steer clear of secondhand mattresses, stuffed animals, pillows, and other items that cannot be thoroughly cleaned and disinfected.

Finally, be safe. If you are meeting a stranger about an item listed online, make sure you meet in a public place. Tell a loved one where you are going beforehand; even better, bring them along with you.

Common Concerns and How to Overcome Them

"But I like new stuff."

I do, too! Know that you can often find new items when you thrift, even ones with tags. Some thrifting websites make it easy for shoppers to filter out older items by clicking the "New" or "Like New" options.

"Do I have to thrift *everything*?"

Sure, if you want to! Or you can thrift specific items. Incrementalism argues that thrifting just a little bit is certainly more eco-friendly than not thrifting at all.

"Aren't gifting and thrifting the opposites of minimalist living?"

They can be, especially if you go overboard. It's important to thrift only for what you need right now and pass on all the items you think you *might* need someday. While refusing good deals requires self-control, it is certainly possible. If you're heading to a brick-and-mortar store, write out a list of what you need before you leave, then stick to the list.

PART 3

The Highest-Hanging Fruit: Self-Sufficiency

CHAPTER 10
Why Self-Sufficiency Matters

In the tail-end of 2019, COVID-19 quietly spread around the world. By March of 2020, it swiftly and silently crippled most nations, both developed and developing. As economies around the world sputtered to a halt, many Americans found themselves facing uncertain futures. Shoppers panicked, abandoning decorum as they cleared supermarket shelves, hoarded supplies, and left little for others.

The terror ushered in by the novel coronavirus pandemic stemmed in large part from the realization that most Americans rely heavily on corporations to provide survival essentials. If grocery stores, gas stations, and other modern conveniences shutter, you're left relying solely on your own ingenuity to survive. It may be sobering to ruminate over how long you can reasonably keep your family fed and warm after the last of your food, water, and oil runs out.

How self-sufficient *are* you, really?

The modern definition of self-sufficiency implies that the notion is intertwined with obtaining gainful employment—you can be considered self-sufficient if you earn a decent salary. But true

For sustainable minimalists, the end goal is not a tidy home, an organized closet, or increased savings in the bank account. The end goal is self-sufficiency.

self-sufficiency is much more than the size of your paycheck, and because self-sufficiency is more adequately defined as the ability to care for daily needs with minimal help, you attain this elusive trait once you've learned essential skills for living. For sustainable minimalists, the end goal is not a tidy home, an organized closet, or increased savings in the bank account. The end goal is self-sufficiency. That's because it's the solution to both over-reliance and overconsumption. Self-sufficiency epitomizes a lifestyle rooted in minimalism because self-sufficient consumers buy less and grow, make, or create more.

There are two ways to become self-sufficient. The first is to drop old and harmful habits, and the second is to learn new, productive skills. In part 1 of this book, you dropped the harmful habits of overbuying and keeping unnecessary items in your living space. In part 2, you adopted new, eco-friendly routines. Part 3 of this book centers on fostering skills that decrease reliance on pollution-producing corporations and overpriced products, for good.

---

10 Self-Sufficient Skills Every Sustainable Minimalist Should Know

1. How to compost

2. How to garden

3. How to preserve food

4. How to cook

5. How to sew and mend

6. How to perform simple home repairs

7. How to make a fire

8. How to store water long-term

9. How to cook without electricity

10. How to forage for wild food

But Why?

Climate scientists warn that floods, droughts, heat waves, and powerful storms will increase in both frequency and intensity in the coming decades.[127] Melting glaciers and rising sea levels will flood coastal towns, and they may remain under water for good. Powerful storms may wipe out our power grids for extended periods of time, and mass migrations of entire nations attempting to escape the consequences of climate change will likely strain communities that are unprepared for the arrival of hundreds of thousands of refugees. Droughts, too, may significantly impact the industrial food system we rely on so heavily.[128]

These days, you and I are a generation or two removed from a crisis. Yet my grandparents and great-grandparents—perhaps yours, too—survived a major economic depression and world wars. As such, they relied on age-old skills (not supermarket conveniences) in difficult times. They understood that self-sufficiency provides security despite uncertainty, and mitigates the stressors associated with sudden illness, job loss, financial setbacks, and more currently, climate change.

While there are many ways to foster self-sufficiency in your daily life, this chapter focuses on just three of the most important: composting, gardening, and preserving food.

Self-Sufficient Skill #1: Compost

Composting ensures that next year's garden has nutrient-rich soil at the ready.

If you're like most Americans, you likely waste a little over 30 percent of your household's food, or $1,866 per year.[129] A slow-but-steady approach to composting reduces food waste because it transforms ho-hum food scraps and produce that's past its prime into nutrient-dense soil for your garden, flower beds, and indoor houseplants. As a self-sufficient skill, composting is the foundation for cultivating a successful garden.

Non-composters often conjure up images of filth, stench, and critters whenever they consider the process. The truth is, outdoor composting is simple. And while it's uncertain whether or not our recycling actually gets recycled, composting ensures that our food scraps and compostable waste stay out of landfills.

You've already set up your three-bin system for trash collection in chapter 6, and now, you'll put it to use. First, start in your kitchen. Set aside fruit, vegetable scraps, and eggshells, and place them in your indoor transport container. Once per day (or whenever your transport container is full), carry the contents to your outdoor compost bin. Fruit and vegetable peels, including apple cores, carrot ends, and cucumber peels, are considered green matter, and that should constitute one-third of your tumbler's contents at all times.

Next, add brown matter. Brown matter is, well, brown. Small pieces of cardboard are considered brown matter, as are dried leaves and other yard waste. Keep your tumbler or homemade compost bin two-thirds filled with brown matter. Add a bit of water to ensure that the contents within remain moist (but not soaking wet).

If you opted for a tumbler, follow its foolproof instructions that explain in which side of the contraption to put your waste, as well as how often to turn the barrel. If you opted to make your own bin, turn it gently once a week with a shovel to ensure that the dirt covers your food scraps. Then sit back, relax, and let nature do its job.

Get Composting!

Composting isn't for just fruit and vegetable scraps. It's entirely possible to compost the following items, too:

- Coffee grounds and paper coffee filters
- Cotton balls and cotton swabs made of 100-percent cotton
- Wine corks
- Stale bread
- Hair and nail clippings
- Pet hair
- Toilet paper, toilet paper rolls, and tissues
- Cardboard
- Paper egg cartons
- Herbs and spices

Self-Sufficient Skill #2: Garden

Gardening is an essential means of connecting you to your food source.

My mother gardened vigorously every summer during my childhood. I remember her kneeling in the soil, hands working the dirt, her spine taking on the roundness of a tortoise shell. And while I learned all about the intricacies of growing food by observing her from afar, I wanted no part of the actual experience.

Gardening wasn't fun as a child—it was dirty, and it took an awful long time for a single item to grow. But my opinion of gardening has evolved, and these days I'm an enthusiastic gardening convert. I now believe gardening is the greatest hobby in the world, primarily because growing your own food epitomizes self-sufficiency. Home gardens save money because, while organic produce is pricey, limiting costs and

maximizing yield enables you to grow organic fruits and
vegetables for less than what you'd pay at the grocery store.
An article in Money.com reported that "A well-maintained
garden yields half a pound of produce per square foot per
growing season," and a six hundred square-foot garden could
churn out three hundred pounds of fresh produce (or about
$600 annually in savings).[130]

Gardening connects you to your food source, too. Once you
realize how long it takes and how hard it can be to grow a
single head of broccoli or just one vine-ripened tomato, you
may find yourself hesitant to waste nary a bite of it. Gardening
also epitomizes the local food movement, as tending a garden
means you have eliminated your need for big-business
produce that has been shipped from other continents.

At its foundation, gardening is an experiment in learning to grow food.

If gardening sounds like an awful lot of work,
consider adjusting your notions of what a
garden must look like. At its foundation,
gardening is an experiment in learning to
grow food. Gardening can simply mean
growing *something*—one thing, even—in the
space you have. Maybe you cultivate a small,
raised bed on your deck, or perhaps you grow
basil, parsley, or mint on your fire escape. My first garden was a
small raised bed on my deck that I filled with sugar snap peas
and green bean vines. The following year, I added a potted
tomato plant to my "garden." The year after that, I started a few
cucumber plants from seeds. Only one survived, so I re-planted
it in an oversized container on my deck.

Start with Microgreens

It is prudent to save more temperamental plants, like cauliflower, melons, and onions, for future growing seasons. Stick to easy plants during your first gardening attempts. Salad greens are notoriously easy to grow, as are peas and green beans. If you've never grown anything before, microgreens may be a practical place to start. Vibrant microgreens first made their appearances in upscale restaurants in the 1980s as garnishes. These days, seasoned chefs and home cooks alike revere these baby seedlings because they are nutrient- and flavor-packed. Indeed, the concentrations of vitamins and phytochemicals in microgreens are four to six times higher than in the leaves of those same plants when mature.[131]

Salad greens, leafy vegetables, and herbs can be grown as microgreens in repurposed plastic containers. Microgreens are a practical choice for growers with space constraints because they can be grown with very little effort on a sunny windowsill. And because you harvest them in just seven to fourteen days, microgreens offer gratification much sooner than mature vegetables.

Other Gardening Tips

In your first growing season, plant fewer plants. While shopping at a garden center can indeed be motivating, you may quickly find yourself swept away by the Brandywine tomatoes, serrano peppers, and heirloom eggplants. View your first garden—and maybe even your second and third—as experiments. Doing so may alleviate potential disappointment if you don't receive as great a yield as you had hoped.

Remember that location is important. Most vegetables do best in full sun, so plant your garden in a place that receives at least six hours of it each day. In order to provide equal sun exposure to all of your plants, place the tallest ones on the north or west sides so that they don't shade smaller ones. And as you become better-versed in gardening, consider growing only items that you can successfully preserve. Lettuces, for example, do not preserve easily. Instead of using precious garden space to grow such items, consider using that space for tomatoes, beans, or other items whose lives can be extended by freezing or canning. We will discuss the ultra-self-sufficient skill of food preservation next.

Finally, be patient with pests, and do not rush to apply insecticides, as such chemicals pollute soil and groundwater. If you must resort to insecticides, use them responsibly. Never apply pesticides in the morning when pollinators are most active, and do so with full knowledge that synthetic, and even many organic and natural pesticides, kill beneficial insects.[132]

Self-Sufficient Skill #3: Preserve Food

Canning preserves food longer than any other preservation method—
for two years on average.

There is something utterly satisfying about serving summer's homegrown green beans at Thanksgiving dinner, and July's blueberries somehow taste especially sweet in winter muffins. Preserving food is both a salient life skill and a powerful way to reduce supermarket over-reliance. While self-sufficiency demands an understanding of how to grow food, it also requires knowledge of how to preserve your summer bounty for the winter months. Preserving both ensures that no food item is wasted and encourages your family to consume healthy, local produce all year long.

While root crops, winter squash, onions, and garlic will last for up to six months when stored in dark, cool locations, all other foods require some form of preservation to last through winter. There are many different ways to preserve food, including the following:

Dry

If cooking with fresh herbs in the summer is a small luxury, intentionally not buying plastic-packaged commercial herbs in the winter is a gigantic win. Air dry the herbs you grow at home by snipping fresh sprigs at the base, tying them together with a rubber band, and hanging them in the kitchen or out in the sun until dry. Then, crumple the leaves and store them in well-marked, lidded glass containers.

Dehydrate

Dehydrating fruits and vegetables removes water but retains flavor. While a dehydrator simplifies the process, the appliance is big, bulky, and not used all that often in day-to-day life. Consider borrowing a dehydrator from a neighbor, or use your oven instead. Cut produce into one-fourth inch slices and place them on a baking sheet lined with silicone. Turn your oven on to its lowest temperature and leave them in for six to eight hours. For small batches, save energy by dehydrating in your toaster oven.

Freeze

There are both benefits and drawbacks to freezing as a means of preserving food. While the process is simple and does not require an expensive gadget, running a freezer expends electricity. And in the event of power loss, you may lose all the food you diligently preserved.

Although food items with high water content like cucumbers, mushrooms, and lettuce do not freeze well, you can freeze many vegetables and fruits, including corn, peas, broccoli, cauliflower, carrots, green beans, berries, and bananas, for up to ten months.

Most vegetables benefit from blanching before freezing. Rinse and cut them as you normally would, and be sure to trim stems and damaged areas. Chop large vegetables into manageable sizes, then them put in boiling water for two to three minutes. Transfer them to an ice bath to halt the cooking process, then pat them dry with a tea towel to prevent freezer burn. Create less waste by storing items in glass jars, metal tins, or silicone bags over plastic bags.

I occasionally freeze herbs, too, by mincing them finely, placing them in ice cube trays, then topping each cube off with a bit of olive oil. Once frozen, I transfer the cubes to a lidded storage container. I then use these individually portioned herbs in soups, stews, and other favorite recipes.

Can

Canning is by far my favorite way to preserve food, and using the pressure canner is a thrilling experience for the entire family each and every time. A pressure canner is a heavy pot with a locking lid and a pressure gauge. As water boils within, pressure builds inside the pot. While Ani and Lara squeal with glee every time the canner steams boisterously, I receive quiet satisfaction from the gentle rocking of the jars within. The minimalist in me loves opening my pantry to orderly lines of uniform mason jars, and because the process enables me to reuse jars again and again for canning purposes, it creates a completely plastic-free and low-waste end product.

Canning is the go-to preservation method for many, and that's because canned foods last much longer than frozen foods— up to two years on average. While you are able to can some items (like jam) safely in a boiling water bath on your stove, many other low-acid foods, including most vegetables, meat, and fish, require a pressure canner for safe preservation, as the high temperatures associated with pressure canning kill harmful microorganisms.[133] Make sure you follow the directions that come with your pressure canner to the letter to ensure the safety of the foods within. If you opt to borrow a pressure canner from a friend, make sure you also have access to its directions. Alternately, ask someone you know who cans regularly whether you can observe and learn.

Real Life Sustainable Minimalists

Obsessed with Food in All the Right Ways

I'm a freelance farmer, so to me, minimalist self-sufficiency means I have the know-how to grow my own food, acquire food items without relying on the supermarket, and cook with the items I have grown and acquired.

I often acquire food by bartering. I have two bins filled with seeds and I trade them for other items such as meat, eggs, and dairy. I also acquire food by accepting gifts. Sometimes my clients share their abundance with me, and I happily accept. I recently made sauerkraut with gifted cabbage. My six-year-old helped, and the process also became a homeschooling lesson.

I believe cooking is a critical life skill. I bake bread from scratch and create veggie stock from scraps. I rely on a water bath canner to can my own tomato sauce, salsa, applesauce, and jams. I also make beef jerky in my dehydrator. If I have extra milk, I make mozzarella and ricotta, yogurt, or cottage cheese before it spoils. These are skills I love and intend to pass onto future generations. They provide teaching opportunities to show others that there are options beyond consumerism.

SARAH EDELMAN, Sustainable Minimalists group member

The Final Word

The process of becoming self-sufficient is an incremental one that should be fun, too.

While learning multiple new skills at once can quickly become overwhelming, viewing self-sufficiency as an attribute that is best attained over time eases that stress. One summer, I acquired a pressure canner and taught myself to can vegetables. Another, I learned how to make bars of soap. Consider committing to learning one new skill every year. By slowing down the process, you give yourself both the time and the freedom to fully immerse yourself in the joys that come with learning something new.

Instead of committing to skills that sound boring or cumbersome, consider creating opportunities to adopt new hobbies you've always wanted to try. Sewing, foraging, tapping for maple syrup, raising chickens, and caring for bees are just some ways to lessen reliance on corporations while also having some good, old-fashioned family fun. Have you always wanted to learn how to knit? Sign up for a class at your local yarn store, or enlist the help of a friend who's an avid knitter. Aim to simply foster a love of a new hobby—the thrill of learning new skills may inspire you to learn more.

Common Concerns and How to Overcome Them

"Composting sounds easy enough, but I have no use for compost."

The main benefit of composting is that it diverts food waste from landfills, so although many home composters don't need their compost, they compost anyway. Consider donating your humus to a local farmer or gardener. Alternately, sign up for municipal composting if your city or town offers it.

"Gardening seems like an expensive hobby. How can I keep costs down?"

If you aren't careful, gardening can get expensive. Don't spend significant money upfront, especially if you aren't sure gardening is a hobby you'll stick with. Budget the most money for quality soil and compost, and budget the least for tools of the trade. Keep your eye out for quality, secondhand tools and netting at garage sales, too, or borrow from a friend.

"My home is small. I don't have a lot of space to store cans upon cans of food."

I would argue that if there is a single item minimalists should keep on hand for that just-in-case event, it's food. Consider storing long-lasting food items in places beyond the kitchen. Do you have a basement? A crawl space under the stairs? How about under your bed? Aim to keep enough extra food on hand for three to six months, and don't feel weird about storing it in unconventional places. Be sure to continuously replenish your stock as you consume it.

CHAPTER 11

DIY for a Life with Less

Making at home what you used to buy at the store saves money and increases self-sufficiency.

Making items you once bought both refines your skill set and reduces your reliance on money-making corporations.

From well-lit, air-conditioned stores to e-commerce, our consumerist society is constantly enticing us to buy every item we need and desire. Yet making instead of buying is an eco-friendly and self-sufficient habit, so despite such convenience, sustainable minimalists happily embrace the do-it-yourself (DIY) lifestyle whenever possible.

Making items you once bought both refines your skill set and reduces your reliance on money-making corporations. You may have already reached a pinnacle moment of clarity when you realized that you don't need half the items corporations sell to you. Absorbing this realization fully and changing your buying habits accordingly is a critical step toward both minimalism and self-sufficiency. There are additional benefits to embracing a DIY lifestyle, including the following:

DIY Is...

Minimalist

Making what you once bought gives you control over what enters your home. And because DIYing requires your time, the practice empowers you to think long and hard about what is essential versus what is not. Many minimalists find joy in creating only the items they truly value and will actually use.

Eco-Friendly

DIY products reduce plastic waste. The plastic bottles you rely on to transport shampoos, lotions, and cleaning products from the store to your home will remain on earth for *at least* the next four and a half centuries,[134] but DIY encourages reuse of products you already have on hand like bottles, jars, and more. And because DIY by definition is made in-house, it is the epitome of the local movement.

Non-Toxic

The only way to know what you are buying is to not buy at all.

The US government shows favoritism toward companies and manufacturers at the expense of consumer health,[135] and the FDA only loosely regulates the chemicals in personal care products. While 62,000 chemicals in personal care products are approved for use in the United States, less than 300 have been tested.[136] The bar for toxic chemical regulation in the US is dramatically lower than it is in the European Union, too: the EU has banned or restricted more than 1,300 chemicals in cosmetics alone, while just 11 are banned in the United States.[137] You may, therefore, be unaware of the sad truth that your body absorbs untested and unsafe chemicals from shampoo and toothpaste, among other things.

Chemicals in store-bought cleaning supplies are similarly concerning. Many staple ingredients are toxins linked to asthma, cancer, and hormonal imbalances. They threaten both the planet and your personal health as they pollute your home's air and water when used in poorly ventilated spaces and washed down your drains.[138]

Enjoyable

Ani loves melting beeswax into candles and giving them as holiday gifts. Lara enjoys shaking the ingredients in DIY dry shampoo with all her might before inadvertently covering herself in cocoa powder.

Because the DIY options listed in this chapter are simple, you will likely not see them as burdensome. Consider batching multiple projects and tackling them all in a single afternoon. Enlist your children's help in the process as a means of both educating and entertaining them.

DIY Task #1: Cleaning Supplies

Cleaning product corporations market the idea that your home must smell like toxic chemicals in order to be clean. And despite both the ease and savings associated with making your own cleansers, you may find yourself shying away from the practice due to concerns that homemade ones don't *actually* disinfect.

Yet there are fundamental differences between cleaning and disinfecting. While cleaning uses

Homemade cleansers clean just as well as commercial ones, and without the questionable chemicals.

soap and removes germs and dirt from surfaces, disinfecting kills germs without necessarily cleaning.[139] Commercial disinfectants that line supermarket shelves do indeed pack a hefty, germ-killing punch, but bringing dangerous chemicals into your home may not be worth the potential health and environmental side effects.

Homemade cleansers generally contain three ingredients in varying amounts: castile soap, white vinegar, and baking soda. **Vinegar** is 5 percent acidic and is a powerful disinfectant that is just as effective at killing some bacteria—including salmonella— as name-brand products.[140] White vinegar dissolves soap scum and removes grime and grease, too. Yet while its acidity makes it a wonder cleanser, vinegar is not suitable for every job. Do not use vinegar on granite or marble countertops, and avoid using it in DIY dishwasher and laundry detergent. Skip the vinegar on wood furniture and flooring, too, as its acidity may eat away at the wood's protective finish.

Whereas vinegar is an acid, **baking soda** is a base. Many homemade cleansers mix baking soda with white vinegar, causing an acid-base reaction and creating a cleaning powerhouse. But baking soda can also stand on its own as a natural odor absorbent and a slightly abrasive scrubbing agent.

Castile soap is a vegetable-based soap that is nontoxic, biodegradable, and available for purchase in bar or liquid form. (When it comes to this soap, I recommend purchasing liquid, as it negates the need for shredding a bar.) Castile soap should never be combined with vinegar or lemon juice, as it will leave behind a white, filmy residue.

Because vinegar, baking soda, and castile soap are relied upon in many DIY cleansers, consider purchasing them in the largest sizes you can find. Although doing so is not a minimalist habit, buying in bulk saves money, limits unnecessary packaging waste, and reduces emissions associated with unnecessary package shipment.

Replace the Most Toxic Products First

Oven Cleaner

Oven cleaners often include sodium hydroxide and butoxydiglycol, chemicals that can blind, burn skin, and kill if ingested.[141] Make your own oven cleaner at home by mixing together equal parts baking soda, salt, and vinegar. Let it soak in the oven for a few hours, then get to scrubbing.

Toilet Bowl Cleaner

Toilet bowl cleaner contains hydrochloric acid and chlorine bleach, both of which are harmful to the lungs when either inhaled or absorbed through the skin.[142] For a safe, DIY alternative, add 1 cup of water, ½ cup of castile soap, and ¼ cup of vinegar to an old dish soap squirt bottle. Next, add ½ cup of baking soda. Put the cover on the bottle and shake until combined. Squirt the cleanser in and around toilet bowl, then let it sit for fifteen minutes before scrubbing clean.

Drain Cleaner

Commercial drain cleaner is unnecessary. Make a vinegar and baking soda solution that naturally dissolves clogs by pouring baking soda in the sink and drizzling vinegar on top. Follow with very hot water. For bigger clogs, use a metal clothes hanger as a drain snake.

Dryer Sheets

Dryer sheets are single-use, disposable items. They contain questionable ingredients, too: research has found twelve harmful chemicals in dryer sheets, including ethanol, chloroform, and benzyl acetate.[143] Lingering chemical residue from dryer sheets and fabric softeners remains on clothes and enters your body through your skin. It directly affects the nervous and endocrine systems, and contributes to the development of chronic illnesses.[144]

Eliminate the need for dryer sheets altogether by laundering differently. In the washing machine, add a scoop of kosher salt with an essential oil of your choice. While the salt helps soften clothes, essential oils add a slight scent. Next, put your clothes in the dryer with a reusable wool dryer ball, and add a drop of essential oil to each ball for fragrance.

Air Freshener

Air fresheners mask odors by emitting artificial chemicals, or phthalates, into the air. Phthalates have been linked to hormonal abnormalities, reproductive problems, and birth defects. By design, air fresheners amplify phthalates' toxicity because they are often used indoors in unventilated rooms.[145]

If you want to make your home smell pleasant without the use of dangerous chemicals, here are five natural ideas:

- Bring home a fragrant, flowering house plant, like jasmine or gardenia.

- Diffuse essential oils in a diffuser.

- Open the windows to allow stale odors to exit.

- Dab a Q-Tip in an essential oil and hide it in your toilet paper roll in the bathroom.

- Place baking soda jars around your home, just as you do in your refrigerator!

Make Simple Cleansers

For everyday jobs, make the following cleansers and store them in repurposed spray bottles.

An All-Purpose Cleanser

Mix equal parts vinegar and water in a spray bottle. (Yes, it's *that* easy!)

If you find the smell of vinegar off-putting, reserve some orange peels and create an all-purpose cleanser infused with citrus. Add the peels to a lidded jar, then add two cups of white vinegar, making sure the vinegar covers all the peels. Let it steep undisturbed and in a shaded spot for three weeks—the longer it steeps, the more citrus-infused the final product will be. After three weeks, use a cheesecloth or strainer to separate the orange peels from the vinegar. Then, mix equal parts citrus vinegar with water in a spray bottle to create your all-purpose cleanser.

If your countertop is made of marble, granite, or stone, mix water with rubbing alcohol or vodka instead of vinegar, as vinegar is too acidic for some countertops.

A Cleanser for Windows and Mirrors

Mix 1 part white vinegar, 4 parts water, and a splash of lemon juice. Instead of wiping with paper towels, use old newspaper.

Reusable "Clorox" Wipes

Mix 1 cup of water, ¼ cup of rubbing alcohol, 1 teaspoon of dish soap, and 2 optional tablespoons of ammonia in a bowl, then soak rags in the solution. Use as you would a normal Clorox wipe, then rinse, wash, and reuse.

Carpet Cleanser

For deep stains, attack with soapy water, vinegar, and a bristle brush, or blot with soda water and a clean rag. For carpet odors, sprinkle baking soda, let it sit, then vacuum it up.

Polish Wood Furniture

Mix 1 cup of vegetable oil with 1 teaspoon of lemon oil, and apply it to furniture with a clean rag.

Pots and Pans Scrub

Mix sea salt with lemon juice into a paste, then scrub away.

Laundry Detergent

Make your own laundry detergent by spreading one pound of baking soda onto a cookie sheet and baking at 400 degrees for forty minutes. Doing so will spike the pH and turn the baking soda into washing soda. (Use caution and do not inhale!) Wait until the baking soda becomes washing soda, then add 2 ounces of castile soap and 20 to 30 drops of your favorite essential oil for scent. When washing clothes, use 2 tablespoons of your DIY detergent per load.

Dish Soap

Add 1 part castile soap to 10 parts water to make liquid dish soap.

DIY Task #2: Beauty Products

Although the beauty industry promises to make us prettier, healthier, and more desirable, the reality is that most beauty products contain questionable ingredients in disposable, plastic containers.

The average American woman uses twelve beauty products per day, which collectively amounts to over one hundred chemicals.[146] Among the most concerning are formaldehyde (found in body soap and nail polish) and coal tar (found in hair dye and shampoo). Lipstick is full of heavy metals, including lead, and endocrine-disrupting parabens and phthalates reside in a host of even more products.[147]

While a single exposure to a toxic chemical probably won't hurt you, over time, these exposures (literally) add up. The concept of "body burden" defines the sum total of all the toxic chemicals that have accumulated in your body over time, and some chemicals have synergistic effects that create an even worse toxin when combined.[148] And because children's systems are undeveloped and their skin is 30 percent thinner than that of adults, they may be particularly vulnerable to the chemicals in everyday products like diaper cream, sunscreen, and baby shampoo.[149]

Clean Beauty?

Know Your Chemicals

Learn to identify the worst-offending chemicals in beauty products, then avoid them.

- Parabens
- Sodium lauryl or laureth sulfate (SLES)
- Fragrance
- Triclosan (TCS)
- Formaldehyde
- Polyethylene glycol (PEG)
- Beta hydroxy/salicylic acid (BHA) & butylated hydroxytoluene (BHT)
- Ethanolamines
- Dibutyl phthalate (DBP) and toluene
- Coal tar dyes
- Hydroquinone
- Oxybenzone

The beauty industry makes many non-toxic claims that are simply false. "Clean" beauty is all the rage these days, and corporations know that health-conscious consumers will spend more money on products they believe are free of unnecessary chemicals. They therefore market their products specifically to such consumers by adding in wording such as "paraben-free" or "free of formaldehyde, BHA, and PEGs." The problem, however, is that a paraben-free product is not necessarily clean, as it may still have other questionable chemicals. And because the FDA very loosely regulates the beauty industry, many products boast fancy (yet untrue) claims that incorrectly boost your confidence in a product's safety.

Hey There, Marketing Gimmicks

Recognize these product descriptors that are actually just marketing ploys:

- Natural
- Organic
- Non-toxic
- Botanical
- Clean
- Hypoallergenic

- Physician-approved
- Simple
- Safe
- Eco-Friendly
- Green

Sustainably Minimize Your Beauty Regimen in Two Steps

There *is* good news: it is entirely possible to clean up your beauty routine in two simple steps.

Step 1: Think like a Minimalist

Thanks in part to behavioral conditioning by the beauty industry, many consumers retain cabinets and drawers overflowing with beauty products. A practical first step to reducing both exposure to chemical-laden products and future packaging waste is to analyze the items you currently have. Could you reasonably live without some products you have traditionally relied on? Consider using a bar of soap instead of shaving cream, for example, as shaving cream often list glycols as a main ingredient, which are linked to kidney damage and blood disorders.[150] And because shaving cream is often packaged in non-recyclable cans, regular usage increases the amount of unnecessary waste your home produces.

Consider, too, whether you could reasonably use some products less often, as doing so reduces the body burden associated with daily use. Instead of wearing nail polish and perfume daily, don these items on special occasions. For products you use every day, is it possible to use half of your normal amount?

Know that some non-toxic beauty items can perform dual functions. Can you replace two chemical-laden products with a single, natural product? Coconut oil, for example, is a wonderful face and body moisturizer, as well as an exceptional makeup remover.

Finally, be sure to try samples before splurging on oversized bottles and containers of products you may not like. For products that you don't like and will no longer use, head to **makeupalley.com**, a platform that enables women to swap products they are displeased with.

Real Life Sustainable Minimalists

Enjoying the Process

Modern society tells us that we must use certain products to be professional, successful, and hygienic. And while personal hygiene *is* important, there are many ways to be hygienic beyond buying products off the shelf. I knew that giving up familiar products might feel awkward and taboo, but I no longer wanted to put unsafe chemicals on my body. I didn't want to create unnecessary trash or support unethical companies, either.

It's easy to grab products off store shelves, but it only takes three minutes to assemble six-month's worth of DIY deodorant and toothpaste at home. I've learned that many DIY products use common household ingredients. I use baking soda to make toothpaste, as well as to bake cookies, clean my floors, and do laundry. I keep my trash to a minimum by buying most ingredients in the bulk section at the grocery store, and refilling the same cloth bags and jars over and over. While I can't always get what I need in a zero-waste format, I do my best to buy the largest quantity with the most recyclable packaging. Although I am buying a packaged product, I can assemble a large batch of products that will create less waste than buying single-use products.

I love being so intimately connected with the process of creating my products and knowing exactly what's in them. Don't be afraid to experiment and enjoy the process!

NATASSJA CASSINERIO, episode #048 podcast guest
hestiaspeaks.com

Step 2: DIY What You Can

Crafting homemade beauty products is truly the "clean" option—when you make items yourself, you know with 100-percent certainty what lies within. And DIYing your beauty regimen enables you to reuse packaging items like jars, old deodorant sticks, and more, which reduces unnecessary packaging waste.

Common ingredients in DIY beauty products include beeswax, coconut oil, and shea butter. Consider buying these items in bulk for greater savings.

Lip Balm

In a microwave-safe container, melt 3 tablespoons of beeswax, 2 tablespoons of shea butter, and 4 tablespoons of coconut oil in thirty-second increments, stirring well after each one. Stir in essential oil, if desired. Carefully pour the mixture into tubes or containers and allow it to cool before using. Consider washing out old eye shadow containers to store your homemade lip balm.

Hand and Body Lotion

Combine ½ cup of olive oil, ¼ cup of coconut oil, and ¼ cup of beeswax in a coffee can atop a double boiler. Add shea butter. Stir occasionally as the ingredients melt. When all the ingredients are completely melted, add 1 teaspoon of Vitamin E and essential oils, if desired. Let it cool. Separate your lotion into baby food jars or another miniature container and leave them in various places throughout your home.

Deodorant

Deodorant and antiperspirant are quite different from each other. While deodorant targets odors, antiperspirant contains aluminum salts that prevent sweat glands from releasing sweat. Clinical studies show a disproportionately high incidence of breast cancer when antiperspirants are topically applied to the underarm.[151] [152] Most conventional products on the market have both deodorant and antiperspirant qualities.

Combine 1 tablespoon of coconut oil, 1 tablespoon of arrowroot powder, 1 tablespoon of shea butter, 1 tablespoon of baking soda, and 1 or 2 drops of lemongrass oil (optional) over a double boiler on the stove or in the microwave. Let it cool. Store the mixture in a jar and apply like lotion to use. Or, if you prefer to reuse an empty deodorant stick, let the texture cool completely before inserting.

Non-Petroleum Jelly

Petroleum jelly is a byproduct of petroleum (or crude oil) and is made from the waxy material that forms on oil rigs after distilling it.[153] It's entirely possible to reap Vaseline's same moisturizing benefits without relying on fossil fuels.

Combine ⅛ cup of beeswax and ½ cup of olive oil in an old coffee can and melt over low heat in a double boiler. Let the mixture cool, and store it inside a repurposed glass jar with a lid.

Dry Shampoo

Place cornstarch in a repurposed jar. Add cocoa powder to tint (dark hair will require more cocoa powder than lighter hair.) Shake to mix. Apply to hair roots using an old makeup brush.

Toothpaste

Mix 2 parts arrowroot powder or baking soda, 1 part coconut oil, and 1 drop of peppermint oil (optional) with a fork. Store the mix in a container that tightly seals. When ready to use, apply it to your toothbrush with a clean spoon.

Daily Facial Products

Raw honey and sugar mixed together make a nice facial exfoliant. Lightly rub the mixture onto your skin and wash it off with warm water. For blemishes, spot treat with diluted tee tree oil, which is powerful against breakouts.

To create your own makeup, consider the following instructions:

Blush

Mix ½ teaspoon of arrowroot powder, ½ teaspoon of organic cocoa powder, and ½ teaspoon of hibiscus powder in a small bowl. Adjust the quantities of each ingredient to achieve your desired shade. Store in a repurposed glass jar and apply with a makeup brush.

Eyeshadow

Mix cocoa powder (brown shades), spirulina (green shades), and arrowroot (light shades) to achieve desired colors.

Eye Liner

Mix ½ ounce each of coconut oil and shea butter in a small bowl, then add ½ teaspoon of activated charcoal. For brown eyeliner, mix coconut oil and shea butter as above, but add cocoa powder instead of activated charcoal. Store in a small jar or repurposed makeup container.

Mascara

Successful homemade mascara uses a handful of obscure (and expensive) ingredients. If you aren't sure whether you'll make mascara often enough to make the initial investment into the recipe's ingredients, consider purchasing a chemical-free commercial option instead.

Mix ¼ teaspoon of black mineral powder, ¼ teaspoon of bentonite clay, ⅛ teaspoon of vegetable glycerin, ¼ teaspoon of aloe vera gel, and 5 drops of lavender essential oil in a bowl until clump-free and smooth. Add more aloe vera gel if needed for consistency. Using a funnel, pour the mixture into a medicine dropper and slowly squirt it into a clean, repurposed mascara container.

Common Concerns and How to Overcome Them

"I already have a lot of cleaning products that are full or nearly full. What do I do with them all?"

As you transition from commercial to homemade cleansers, I suggest not throwing out your current products and starting over, as doing so is stressful, unaffordable, and the opposite of incremental. Instead, slowly replace products with homemade alternatives as they run out. Pay special attention to the most dangerous cleansers and replace them with safer, DIY alternatives first.

"I just don't have time to DIY everything."

Me either! DIYing everything is daunting, and doing so often comes at the expense of enjoying other hobbies. Instead of making *everything* yourself, only make the items you use most often. Alternately, consider making the items that you consider to be the most fun to create.

"I'm not interested in making my own cleansers and beauty products, but I am interested in purchasing items without questionable ingredients. Are there any resources for me?"

Although consumers have the responsibility to support companies committed to doing things right, it can be difficult to actually *find* these companies. I recommend heading to the **Environmental Working Group** website (ewg.org). The EWG is a nonprofit health and advocacy group with product databases that rate commercial cleaning and beauty products based on their ingredients. While the databases are not comprehensive, they are a solid starting point for conscious consumers.

"Is there a way to find products that are sustainably packaged?"

While there is no database to date that lists thoughtfully packaged cleaning and beauty products, a few rules making shopping for eco-conscious products easier. Look for products that have no packaging at all (such as a bar of soap instead of liquid soap, or a shampoo bar instead of a bottle of shampoo). For packaged items, prioritize compostable packaging and seek out products with the fewest unnecessary packaging elements—a plastic container wrapped in a box that is wrapped in a layer of plastic film, for example, has far too many components to be considered sustainable.

CHAPTER 12

Become a Change-Maker

I'm a worrier.

In the short term I worry that, despite recent shifts in popular opinion, the political pull of the fossil fuel industry will prevent meaningful environmental change from taking off.

But in the long term? Science informs us that by 2050, intense droughts will significantly disrupt both global agriculture and water supply.[154] Other extreme weather events—including massive hurricanes and crippling snow storms—will become commonplace. I wonder what such a constant, day-to-day barrage will do to societies around the globe. The very rich, within their fortified and air-conditioned homes, will be able to weather extreme heat, lack of essential resources, and conflicts stemming from mass migrations. The rest of humanity, however, will likely be left to duke it out. As is often the case, the poorest will likely suffer the most, despite having contributed to climate change the least.

It has never been more important for you and I to step up as change-makers. Change-makers do all that they can as sustainable minimalists within their homes, yes, but they also work tirelessly outside of their homes to both educate and inspire others about the benefits of simpler, reduction-based lifestyles. Change-makers understand that, while caring about the environment may be a privilege, the environment is for everyone. As such, change-makers are consciously inclusive because they know the movement will only succeed if it includes people with distinct voices, diverse skin colors, and varied life experiences.

This chapter outlines eight ways you can become a sustainable minimalist change-maker, with four ideas specifically for parents who aspire to raise the next generation of environmental stewards.

Get Loud

Support candidates who make environmental issues their first thought instead of an afterthought.

Legislation that puts the planet over profit has the power to significantly alter the course of Earth's future. While it's unlikely that *global* environmental change will happen from within your household, your civic engagement can create change. Perhaps the most impactful way you can ignite such change is to be a loud, informed citizen who is passionate about the democratic process. Watch televised debates between candidates with your family, then discuss what you heard. Attend community forums, picket peacefully when appropriate, and head to the ballot box and vote in both local and national elections. Consider volunteering your time, energy, and finances to your preferred political candidates, too, if you're able.

Support candidates who make environmental issues their first thought instead of an afterthought. Be sure to support measures that support resiliency, such as improving aging infrastructure, strengthening health care services, and advocating for environmental justice for all people.

Pay special attention to what is happening in the marginalized communities near you. One of the most troubling aspects of environmental injustice is that instances don't get the attention of the mainstream media until something terrible happens, and environmental injustice happens every single day. Don't wait for the mainstream media to tell you about it. Seek it out instead, then say something.

Get loud in other, smaller ways, too. A few years ago, when Kleenex came out with their newest product—disposable hand towels—I wrote a strongly worded letter to the company voicing my criticisms. And when I realized that my beloved exercise studio offered only bottled water to patrons, I said something.

While my letter to Kleenex went unanswered, my exercise studio ultimately phased out water bottles entirely over the course of six months.

Your biggest asset is your loud voice. Stand up and speak out by contacting companies and businesses every single time something doesn't seem quite right from an eco-conscious standpoint. Put your money where your mouth is, too, by consciously choosing to not support bad actors.

Your Customizable Template

Having trouble putting thoughts on paper? Use the template below as your starting point, then customize it to meet your needs.

To Whom it may Concern:

My name is [your name here] and I have been a customer of [company name here] for [duration]. Over the years, I have particularly enjoyed [x, y, z products/services]. However, your eco-harmful packaging and policies have recently led me to become wary of your brand.

While I adore your [product/service], I've noticed that [be specific here. Examples: "Your products contain excessive plastic packaging," "You give out free plastic water bottles during spin class," or "All your products are single-use disposables"].

Plastic takes approximately 450 years to decompose. Worse, it pollutes our oceans and kills our wildlife. Single-use items in your product line such as [list specific products] require excessive energy to produce and are unnecessarily wasteful.

Your [policies and/or packaging] are highly detrimental to our shared planet.

My purchasing decisions are informed by my environmental concerns. Do you have plans to make your business policies more eco-friendly? I'd love to continue supporting [company name here] if your policies adapt to reflect sustainability.

I look forward to hearing from you.

Sincerely,
[your name here]

Bring the Problem to Others

Unfortunately, the environment is a polarizing topic in today's hyper-political environment. But although climate change is considered by many to be a partisan issue, it shouldn't be. In the instances when friends, family, and even strangers engage out of genuine curiosity, seize the opportunity to both teach and inspire. Guide conversations away from politics and toward the reality that the environment is for everyone, regardless of political affiliation.

When teaching others, remember that humanity tends to be more concerned about *visible* environmental problems. The public views polluted drinking water, rivers, and lakes, soil contamination, and ocean and beach pollution as more troublesome than the lofty, largely unseen problem of climate change. Make environmental issues tangible by focusing conversations on problems others can see, smell, or touch.

Climate change has wide-reaching effects and will impact many areas of public interest, including the economy, human health, social issues, and national security. Connecting environmental issues to ones others are passionate about is a powerful way to dispel the notion that it's possible to ignore climate change. Be sure to integrate the environmental angle into conversations when appropriate, and make the connection explicit.

Your Talking Points Cheat Sheet

Connect the problem of climate change to specific hot-button issues, including the following:

Business and the Economy

- Global warming will likely slash up to a tenth of the gross domestic product by 2100, which is more than double the losses of 2008's Great Recession.[155]

- Warmer temperatures, sea level rise, and extreme weather will damage the agriculture, forestry, and tourism industries. As for trade and supply chains, damage to other countries around the globe will also affect US businesses.

Human Health

- Although effects vary by age, gender, geography, genetics, and socioeconomic status, more people will die from temperature-related illnesses as the planet warms.

- Increased precipitation will spur the proliferation of insects that spread dangerous and deadly diseases like Zika, West Nile, dengue fever, and more.

- Crop declines could lead to undernutrition, hunger, and higher food prices. Excess carbon in the air may make staple crops like barley and soy less nutritious, too.[156]

- More heat may mean longer allergy seasons, as increased rain leads to more mold and fungi.

- Higher temperatures and more extreme events will likely affect the cost of energy, air and water quality, and human comfort and health in cities.

Social Issues

- Trauma from extreme climate-related disasters may lead to and exacerbate mental health issues like anxiety, depression, and suicide.

National Security

- Sea level rise may flood parts of military bases along America's East and Gulf coasts for up to three months per year as soon as 2050.[157]

- National security may be further weakened by climate change, as much of America's critical infrastructure is at risk of flooding from sea level rise. Airports on coasts, docks, and certain railways and highways are particularly at risk.

- Frequent power outages will cripple businesses, hospitals, transportation systems, and more.

Understand Your Skillset

Volunteering for a cause you care about is a great way to meet like-minded people, combat eco-anxiety, and create tangible change. Still, it's incorrect to assume we can all best serve in the same way.

I'm not so deft with my hands, nor do I consider myself a passionate protester. Instead, I volunteer for the environmental movement in my capacity as a podcast host, because my chatty personality translates well to a weekly show.

Each of us has specific and unique skills that can further the environmental movement. Instead of feeling the pull to do all the things all the time, defer to tasks that complement your unique skillset.

Know Thyself

Different personalities are best suited for different tasks, including the following:

Protestor

You are: Guided by a strong sense of right versus wrong.

You are best suited to: Attending rallies, picketing, and distributing literature.

Connector

You are: Charismatic, inspiring, and sociable.

You are best suited to: Bringing people together by introducing others, and facilitating connections among people.

Inquirer

You are: A strategic thinker who thirsts for knowledge and intellectual challenges.

You are best suited to: Spearheading research-related tasks through which you uncover all sides of a problem, as well as the problem's potential solutions.

Communicator

You are: An influential public speaker.

You are best suited to: Leading meetings, writing letters, and conveying ideas in a clear, solution-focused manner.

Builder

You are: Hands-on.

You are best suited to: Tasks that enable you to talk less and do more, such as building what needs to be built or cleaning what needs to be cleaned.

Focus on Small Wins

Society often emphasizes big ideas, big dreams, and big plans. And while oversized innovations certainly hold rank in the environmental movement—lofty aspirations like saving the oceans and banning straws are quite enticing—small successes have their place, too. A volunteer who sees their efforts translate into success is much more likely to sign up for another endeavor.

Instead of dedicating yourself to international causes, consider looking within your own community first. Last year, my town proposed selling a 50-acre parcel of land to a developer for a new housing community. After attending community forums, sitting in at special meetings, and picketing peacefully, voters shot down the proposal at a town-wide special election. That tangible success on a small scale gave me newfound hope about the power individuals have to make a difference. What small-scale environmental issues are happening within your town or city? How can you apply your unique skills and help?

Have children? Older kids and teenagers are motivated by small wins, too. Encourage your older child to take on curated projects like chairing a beach cleanup, starting a home composting system for the entire family, or spearheading a bottle drive at school. Experiencing wins on a small scale may translate into the enthusiasm necessary to delve deeper.

Parent-Specific Tips

The next generation will inherit a destabilized planet, and there has never been a more critical time to become change-makers who teach our children about minimalism, sustainability, and self-sufficiency.

While eco-consciousness is a powerful gift that parents can instill in children as they grow, it can often feel as though teaching them without terrifying them is unachievable. I often ask my podcast guests how they incorporate the tenets of sustainable minimalism into their parenting. Many report that because environmental issues matter to them personally, they believe their children will naturally grow into eco-conscious adults. Your kids may not always listen to what you say, but they're always watching what you do.

Right?

This argument has merit, as many children mature and often do embody some of their parents' ideals. But while it is certainly true that children are watching, it is also true that they are learning from peers, advertisements, and deeply ingrained societal norms. If we as parents are to assume that our children naturally adopt the ideals to which they are exposed, then it must also be the case that our single-use culture, with its emphasis on overconsumption, will similarly influence the trajectory of their respective maturations.

Further, such varied sources of information send conflicting messages that likely confuse children. It is therefore vital to be active in teaching minimalism, sustainability, and self-sufficiency to your kids. Here are four ways to both show and explicitly teach the tenets of sustainable minimalism to children of all ages.

Personalize the *Why*

Ani can sort her trash correctly when she's motivated. She knows *how* to recycle and compost. Still, I recently found perfectly recyclable paper and compostable apple cores in the garbage can. While Ani understood the technical steps related to sorting trash, I realized that she wasn't fully on board. She wasn't *invested*.

Ani—and most children, for that matter—would be more likely to consistently adopt environmentally responsible behaviors if she understood why such behaviors are important. So I took her along on a quick errand to the recycling center. I let her throw glass bottles down the chute until they crashed below, just as I did as a child. The lesson continued the following week: Ani watched from the front yard as the garbage truck trundled down the road, stopped in front of our house, and hoisted our sorted items into the back. Much later, Ani asked what happened to everything that did not get recycled. This ushered a conversation about landfills and the problems associated with waste.

Personalizing the "why" is a powerful way to make eco-conscious habits stick. If your child prefers seafood at dinner, connect that to the concept of clean waterways: pollution-free oceans will enable them to continue to eat favored foods. Or if your children love skiing, they may be more invested in curbing global warming if they internalize the reality that a warming planet will result in significantly shorter ski seasons.

Foster a Love of Nature

Research has documented the benefits of the great outdoors for decades. Outdoor play improves physical health, strengthens bones and muscles, prevents obesity, and builds vitamin D in the body, the latter of which reduces the likelihood of chronic diseases.[158] And because children are more likely to be inventive outdoors, extended time outside improves cognitive and social/emotional development by providing opportunities for planning, prioritizing, troubleshooting, and negotiating.[159]

There's another, lesser-known benefit to spending time outdoors: if your children love the planet, they will more likely fight for it. Consider making unstructured playtime outside a nonnegotiable part of their daily schedules. Doing so will encourage childhoods that overflow with simple pleasures like exploring the neighborhood creek, turning over rocks, and using fallen trees as balance beams. While young children will enthusiastically embark on scavenger hunts and other gross motor adventures, teenagers could conduct independent, interest-led inquiries into the workings of the natural world.

While it can be tempting to skip outdoor play on days when the weather is not cooperating, children who engage in risky play become resilient.[160] Rain and snow have real and perceived risks, and these risks create opportunities to extend your child's physical skills, as well as their confidence. Adopting a rain-or-shine approach encourages your child to experience the uniqueness of each season, which is critical in creating strong bonds with nature.

Play Eco-Games

Lara and Ani love playing games; they also love winning. At bath time, we work together to conserve water by marking the water level on the side of the tub with a washable crayon, then committing to using less water at the next bath. And every night at dinner, eating one's entire meal earns induction to the Clean Plate Club, complete with a special after-dinner treat.

When teaching sustainability to your young children, keep it lighthearted by incorporating interactive games that hold their interest and foster life skills like cooperation and teamwork.

Tailor the competition level based on whether or not your children are motivated by the concepts of winning and losing.

Here are some examples of sustainability-related games that you can play in your home:

- Label yourselves the Green Team and walk around the neighborhood, picking up litter as you go.

- Set a timer and sort the garbage. See how many items can be sorted into the trash, recycling, and compost bins in a set amount of time.

- Make DIY items together.

- Create artwork and homemade instruments using recyclables as a means of educating them on the importance of reuse.

- Collect rainwater in buckets. Which area outdoors collects the most amount of water? (Hint: under a downspout.)

- Spearhead a nature scavenger hunt, complete with a checklist to cross off found items (e.g., feather, wildflower, etc.).

Real Life Sustainable Minimalists

For Their Futures

After my first son was born, I suffered from uncontrollable postpartum anxiety (PPA), and I specifically worried over my baby's future on Earth. Articles about our destruction of the environment, plastic waste, and losing biodiversity knocked me over for days, even though I never really cared about any of it before. When I reached the other side of PPA, I knew I needed to do something, so I started shifting our lives and our consumption. I started by cutting out anything made unethically, and it grew from there. We stopped buying new. We pared down our consumption of meat. We changed our approach to gifting at birthdays and holidays.

You don't have to be perfect to make a real difference. While I knew the changes we were making would help my son's future, I had no idea how much better it would make our lives in the present. We started a garden to grow our own vegetables and herbs, and the garden has been an amazing teaching tool for our kids. We joined our local Buy Nothing group to cut down on our own waste and avoid shopping, and now we know most of our neighbors. We armed ourselves with reusable items like unpaper towels and unsponges, and now we save money because we aren't rebuying basics. We decided to give just three gifts at Christmas, and we spend much less time tidying as a result. Shifting away from that constant churn of consumerism where every holiday, trip, and memory is about getting stuff gave me so much freedom as a mom to think creatively about what these moments really mean to us.

You don't have to be perfect to make a real difference. Practicing sustainable minimalism provides constant opportunities to learn how to be creative, empathetic, and more aware of the effects of our actions on others. I feel proud that my kids already know so much more about how to be stewards to the planet than I did as an adult. I think my focus on the environment has made me a much better mom. That alone makes it worth it.

BARBARA ALFEO, episode #100 podcast guest
sunshineguerrilla.com

Channel Eco-Anxiety in a Healthy Way

Thanks in part to the youth climate movement, pop culture, and apocalyptic media headlines, children are more attuned than ever to looming environmental uncertainty. And while it is important that children understand the implications of climate change on their futures, 57 percent of American teenagers said that climate change made them feel scared and 52 percent said it made them feel angry, with only 29 percent optimistic about the future of the planet.[161]

The American Psychological Association (APA) first defined eco-anxiety in 2017 as "the fear of environmental doom." And as climate protests, heatwaves, and a barrage of natural disasters increase the media's coverage of climate change, mental health studies have reported a surge in children and teenagers with stress, depression, or anxiety over the state of the planet.

Have Fact-Based Conversations

Parents often find it difficult to initiate conversations about climate change with their children. Should you be fully truthful with vulnerable children, or should you instead downplay the science in an effort to shield them from difficult realities?

Successful conversations about climate change start when parents listen more than they speak. Hear out your child's concerns, then ask clarifying questions. Shy away from hyperbole and take pains to avoid imparting undue alarmism. Present the science in plain language, and use words that are both age-appropriate and factual. Instill hope by assuring your child that there are many smart people working hard to fix our planet's problems, and end the conversation by shifting from emotion to action by suggesting actions the family can adopt to help.

What to Say

Together with educators and psychologists, National Public Radio (NPR) put together the following fact-based script[162] to discuss climate change with children as young as four or five:

Humans are burning lots and lots of fossil fuels for energy, in planes, in cars, to light our houses, and that's putting greenhouse gases into the air. Those gases wrap around the planet like a blanket and make everything hotter.

A hotter planet means bigger storms, it melts ice at the poles so oceans will rise, it makes it harder for animals to find places to live.

And it's a really, really big problem, and there are a lot of smart people working hard on it, and there's also lots that we can do as a family to help.

Be Solutions-Oriented

Instead of letting eco-anxiety fester in our children, we can help them channel planet-related fears into action by viewing such fears as a collective energy instead of an ailment.

The most impactful way to help is to focus on solutions. Instead of letting eco-anxiety fester in our children, we can help them channel planet-related fears into action by viewing such fears as a collective energy instead of an ailment. We can use eco-anxiety as a means to teach sustainability—protesting peacefully, campaigning for preferred political candidates, contacting companies that are behaving badly, and supporting the youth climate movement are powerful ways to make a difference on a larger scale.

Discuss environmental success stories, too. Be on the lookout for environmental policies and movements that have succeeded in mitigating pollution or conserving resources. Doing so will help children envision a future that is shaped by their action while also preventing them from descending into inaction due to fear.

Common Concerns and How to Overcome Them

"We live in an urban environment. There isn't much opportunity for unstructured outdoor time."

It can be challenging for city dwellers to create connections with nature; still, it's possible. Prioritize outdoor play at playgrounds, and seek out green spaces like parks and rooftop gardens. If circumstances allow, take weekend trips out of the city to further expose your children to the natural world. Jaunts to the beach, a nearby lake, into the woods, or on an overnight camping trip will further enable them to experience the outdoors firsthand.

"I want to verbalize my values to my kids, but I don't want to indoctrinate, either."

Overly pushy parents can turn children off. If you're worried about sounding too preachy, use "I" statements instead of "you should" ones. Be aware of your own intensity and keep discussions centered around ethics, not talking points! Finally, aim to have two-way conversations, not lectures, as a means of empowering your children to form their own opinions and find their own solutions.

Renewed Hope

I was sitting on the porch, reading by the fading evening light, when I heard Ani and her best friend sprint up the basement stairs.

"Turn off the light," I heard Ani say in her sing-song voice. "We shut them off when we leave a room."

From where I sat, I couldn't see her friend's reaction, but I did hear the slight click of the light switch.

They darted down the hall, then the side door slammed. As the girls found their way to the backyard to continue their playdate, I put down my book. Their interaction at the top of the basement stairs was quick—just three seconds, maybe—and then it was over. But still. I sat with my thoughts as I looked out at the sun setting over the pines.

Sustainable minimalism is a journey, not a destination, and you may very likely never find yourself fully satisfied. Perhaps you will never finish simplifying your life, perhaps you will never achieve a carbon-neutral existence. That apple tree will never be picked bare.

But our actions, thoughts, and words influence those around us. We are all connected, and your eco-conscious efforts within your home fuse with mine. Our personal choices to desire less and live gentler existences are buoyed by the efforts of other like-minded people. Together, we create ripples of change that extend further than we could ever begin to quantify.

I believe sustainable minimalism provides renewed hope for my children and for yours.

Acknowledgements

Before sitting down to write this book, I had idyllic expectations of the process that included a silent working space, minimal (if any!) setbacks, and copious amounts of black coffee.

But then, COVID-19. I wrote as I homeschooled and podcasted. I stole minutes here and there in the hopes of tapping out a few words. I woke up early—too early, if I'm honest—to write when the house was quiet. Thank you to everyone who supported me and therefore made this book possible.

To Haig, for knowing this book should be written and for believing I was the perfect person to write it.

To Ani and Lara, for going with the flow as I descended into the basement to hunch over my computer.

To my first readers for being simultaneously supportive and brutal.

To everyone at Mango who believed in the book's message, and especially to my editor, Natasha Vera, who said from the get-go that she wanted my writing of this book to be enjoyable. Thanks to your guidance, it absolutely was.

To Stuart Beeby, for photographing both my home and me in the best possible light.

To my friends and fellow sustainable minimalists who so willingly wrote the testimonials within the book, including Rose

Lounsbury, Natassja Cassinerio, Laura Durenberger, Melissa Russell, Amanda Warfield, and Barbara Alfeo.

To listeners of *The Sustainable Minimalists* podcast, who so willingly shared their journeys within the pages of this book as well.

Finally, thank you to my dear readers and podcast listeners who are willing to be both countercultural and contrarian. I'm inspired by each of you. Thank you for encouraging your friends and family to check this book out from the library, for passing your copy on to others, and for leaving book reviews on Amazon.

In my experience, aspiring sustainable minimalists benefit from connections with others on the same life journey. Have questions? Contact me at mamaminimalist.com, tag me on your #sustainableminimalists journey, or message me on Instagram @mommyminimalist.

About the Author

Stephanie Seferian believes incremental minimalism is the key to saving our planet.

She is the host of *The Sustainable Minimalists Podcast*, where she offers weekly actionable content that inspires listeners to incorporate slow-but-steady tweaks toward sustainability into their daily lives. Her podcast focuses on demystifying the tenets of sustainable minimalism like eco-friendly parenting, conscious consumerism, and responsible decluttering.

Stephanie is a guest lecturer at the University of Arizona and has been featured by numerous media outlets including *Reader's Digest*, NBC News, *SELF Magazine*, and more.

Appendix

Responsible Decluttering for Every Item

Athletic Shoes

For sneakers in wearable condition, donate them to Goodwill (goodwill.org) or wherever you make clothing donations.

For worn athletic shoes, send them to Nike's recycling facility in Memphis, Tennessee. Nike's Reuse-a-Shoe program (nike.com/sustainability) takes old, worn tennis shoes and grinds them up into a base material for new athletic shoes. Know that Nike only takes athletic shoes—no sandals, boots, or cleats.

Books

Your local library may sell unwanted books at fundraisers, or incorporate them into their existing collection.

Cellular Phones

Drop off your old phones, batteries, and accessories such as headsets, phone chargers, and pagers at your local cell phone chain, or mail them in.

DVDs

DVDs to the Troops (facebook.com/DVDSTOTHETROOPS/) is a nonprofit organization that sends unwanted movies to soldiers abroad. Email them with the number of DVDs you would like to donate at info@dvdstothetroops.org.

Eyeglasses

OneSight (onesight.org) will happily take them, as will LensCrafters (lenscrafters.com) and Pearle Vision (pearlevision.com).

Foreign Currency

UNICEF's Change for Good program (unicefusa.org) will happily take foreign coins and notes as a donation to support its mission.

Kitchen Gadgets

Goodwill and the Salvation Army (salvationarmyusa.org) accept appliances and housewares in solid working order.

Linens

Goodwill and the Salvation Army accept full sets in good condition. For sets that are ripped or stained, repurpose the fabric into picnic blankets, trunk liners for your car, rags, and more.

Magazines

If you have children, save a few for arts and crafts projects. Then inquire as to whether nursing or retirement homes in your area distribute them to residents as reading material.

Medical Supplies

First, inquire whether the hospital or clinic from which you received the item will take it back. If not, get creative: check with your local senior center, churches, rehabilitation facilities, and shelters.

Both Goodwill and the Salvation Army accept wheelchairs, crutches, walkers and scooters.

Crutches 4 Africa (crutches4africa.org) collects gently used mobility devices, crutches, wheelchairs, walkers, and even prosthetic limbs and distributes them to those with physical challenges in Africa.

MedShare (medshare.org) accepts new or gently used durable medical equipment and fully functional biomedical devices.

Musical Instruments

Public school music departments are notoriously underfunded. As such, your local school district may accept your unneeded musical instruments. Offer them to local places of worship, too.

Game Consoles

Nintendo's Take Back Program fixes up and sells old consoles, and recycles old parts sustainably. Request a shipping label by emailing takebackprogram@noa.nintendo.com.

Gamers Outreach (gamersoutreach.org) currently accepts games donations.

Pens

Recycle pens, pencils, markers, and highlighters by sending them directly to TerraCycle (terracycle.com), or mail your old pens, pencils, markers, and highlighters to The Pen Guy, a.k.a. Costas Schuler (penguyart.com). He collects old writing utensils to create recycled art. To date, he has repurposed over 500,000 pens.

Power Cords

BestBuy (bestbuy.com) accepts electronic donations at their retail locations. They take cords, too.

Stuffed Animals

Your local animal shelter may use your stuffed animals as toys for their dogs and cats. Your local police station may give your stuffed animals to children as comfort in the event of an emergency, too.

Tools

Your local Goodwill or Salvation Army accepts hand tools and small power tools.

Habitat for Humanity's Habitat ReStore program (habitat.org/
restores) relies on donations of both hand and power tools,
and picks up large items from your home.

Vases

Your local florist may take vases for reuse in
future arrangements.

VHS Tapes

VHS tapes are notoriously difficult to discard—although the
exterior is plastic, toxic metal lies within. Earth911 (search.
earth911.com) gives a list of recycling locations nearby based
on your zip code.

Wedding Dresses

If your dress is less than five years old, Brides Across America
(bridesacrossamerica.com) will accept it. They gift gowns and
gown accessories to members of the American military and
first responders.

If you have a dress that is more than five years old, contact your
local thrift store and inquire as to whether they accept wedding
gowns (many do).

Wire Hangers

Your local dry cleaner may happily accept hangers for reuse.

Ethical Clothing Brands in the United States

Aliya Wanek

Mata Traders
Osei-Duro
Christy Dawn
Della
Girlfriend Collective
Pact
People of Leisure
Eileen Fisher
Toad&Co

Plus Size

Alice Alexander
Gaia Conceptions

Activewear

Fibre Athletics
ShareHope
Patagonia

Underwear and Lingerie

Blue Canoe
Boody
Wama
Uye Surana
Pansy

Baby and Children

Little Lentil
Wild Dill
Beru Kids

Endnotes

1 Jamie Ducharme, "A Lot of Americans Are More Anxious Than They Were Last Year, a New Poll Says," Time, May 8, 2018, https://www.time.com/5269371/americans-anxiety-poll/.

2 "Facts and Statistics," Anxiety and Depression Association of America, accessed 2020, https://www.adaa.org/about-adaa/press-room/facts-statistics.

3 Aimee Picchi, "Here's a Top Reason Americans are Carrying an Average Credit Card Balance of over $6,200," USA Today, February 12, 2020, https://www.usatoday.com/story/money/2020/02/12/credit-card-debt-average-balance-hits-6-200-and-limit-31-000/4722897002/.

4 "Consumer Expenditures in 2017," US Bureau of Labor Statistics, April 2019, https://www.bls.gov/opub/reports/consumer-expenditures/2017/home.htm.

5 Minter, Adam, Secondhand: Travels in the New Global Garage Sale. Bloomsbury 2019.

6 Mary MacVean, "For Many People, Gathering Possessions Is Just the Stuff of Life," Los Angeles Times, March 21, 2014, https://www.latimes.com/health/la-xpm-2014-mar-21-la-he-keeping-stuff-20140322-story.html.

7 Margot Adler, "Behind the Ever-Expanding American Dream House," National Public Radio, July 4, 2006, https://www.npr.org/templates/story/story.php?storyId=5525283.

8 Dafna Goor et al., "The Imposter Syndrome from Luxury Consumption," Journal of Consumer Research 46, no. 6 (April 2020): 1031–1051.

9 Encyclopedia Britannica Online, "Denis Diderot," by Robert Niklaus, last modified October 1, 2020, https://www.britannica.com/biography/Denis-Diderot.

10 Denis Diderot, "My Old Dressing Gown," trans. Iain Bamforth, PN Review 138 vol. 27, no. 4 (March/April 2001): 5–7.

11 Brianna Wiest, "The 'Diderot Effect' Explains Why It's so Easy to Feel like You Never Have, or Do, Enough," Forbes, July 10, 2018, https://www.forbes.com/sites/briannawiest/2018/07/10/the-diderot-effect-explains-why-its-so-easy-to-feel-like-you-never-have-or-do-enough/.

12 Grolier Encyclopedia, "History of Television," by Mitchell Stephens, accessed 2020, https://stephens.hosting.nyu.edu/History%20of%20Television%20page.html.

13 Louise Story, "Anywhere the Eye Can See, It's Likely to See an Ad," The New York Times, January 15, 2007, https://www.nytimes.com/2007/01/15/business/media/15everywhere.html.

14 Sander van der Linden, "The Psychology of Competition," Psychology Today, June 24, 2015, https://www.psychologytoday.com/us/blog/socially-relevant/201506/the-psychology-competition.

15 Francesca Donner, "The Household Work Men and Women Do, and Why," The New York Times, February 12, 2020, https://www.nytimes.com/2020/02/12/us/the-household-work-men-and-women-do-and-why.html.

16 Lucia Ciciolla and Suniya S. Luthar, "Invisible Household Labor and Ramifications for Adjustment: Mothers as Captains of Households," Sex Roles 81, no. 7-8 (October 2019): 467-486.

17 Megan Leonhardt, "Here's How Much Debt Americans Have at Every Age," CNBC, August 20, 2018, https://www.cnbc.com/2018/08/20/how-much-debt-americans-have-at-every-age.html.

18 Leo Sun, "A Foolish Take: Here's How Much Debt the Average U.S. Household Owes," USA Today, November 18, 2017, https://www.usatoday.com/story/money/personalfinance/2017/11/18/a-foolish-take-heres-how-much-debt-the-average-us-household-owes/107651700/.

19 John Gathergood, "Debt and Depression: Causal Links and Social Norm Effects," The Economic Journal 122, no. 563 (September 2012): 10941144.

20 National Geographic Resource Library, "Nonrenewable Resources," accessed 2020 https://www.nationalgeographic.org/encyclopedia/nonrenewable-resources/.

21 Christina Nunez, "Fossil Fuels, Explained," National Geographic, April 2, 2019, https://www.nationalgeographic.com/environment/energy/reference/fossil-fuels/.

22 "Basic Information About Landfill Gas," Landfill Methane Outreach Program
    (LMOP), United States Environmental Protection Agency, accessed
    [insert date here], https://www.epa.gov/lmop/basic-information-
    about-landfill-gas.

23 Syed R. Qasim and Walter Chiang, Sanitary Landfill Leachate: Generation,
    Control and Treatment (Florida: CRC Press, 1994) 245.

24 Michael Balter, "The Origins of Tidiness," Science Magazine, December 18,
    2009, https://www.sciencemag.org/news/2009/12/origins-tidiness.

25 Alice Boyes, "6 Benefits of an Uncluttered Space," Psychology Today, February
    12, 2018, https://www.psychologytoday.com/us/blog/in-
    practice/201802/6-benefits-uncluttered-space.

26 Sarah Berger, "Here's How Much Time Homeowners Spend on Housework
    Compared to Renters," CNBC, September 21, 2018, https://www.
    cnbc.com/2018/09/21/apartment-list-time-owners-spend-
    on-housework-compared-to-renters.html.

27 Mark Bittman, "A No-Frills Kitchen Still Cooks," The New York Times, May 9,
    2007, https://www.nytimes.com/2007/05/09/dining/09mini.html.

28 J. Kenji López-Alt, "The Food Expiration Dates You Should Actually Follow,"
    The New York Times, April 15, 2020, https://www.nytimes.com/article/
    expiration-dates-coronavirus.html.

29 Jason Marsh, "How to Help Kids Learn to Love Giving," Greater Good
    Magazine, December 14, 2016, https://www.greatergood.berkeley.
    edu/article/item/how_to_help_kids_learn_to_love_giving.

30 Nathaniel Meyersohn, "How the Rise of Supermarkets Left out Black
    America," CNN Business, June 16, 2020, https://www.cnn.
    com/2020/06/16/business/grocery-stores-access-race-inequality/
    index.html.

31 "Are Hybrid Cars Worth It?" Autolist, July 24, 2019, https://www.autolist.com/
    guides/are-hybrid-cars-worth-it.

32 Denise Lu, "We Would Need 1.7 Earths to Make Our Consumption
    Sustainable," The Washington Post, May 4, 2017, https://www.
    washingtonpost.com/graphics/world/ecological-footprint/.

33 Neil Irwin, "Climate Change's Giant Impact on the Economy: 4 Key Issues,"
    The New York Times, January 17, 2019, https://www.nytimes.
    com/2019/01/17/upshot/how-to-think-about-the-costs-of-climate-

change.html.

34 National Geographic Resource Library, "Nonrenewable Resources."

35 Irina Ivanova, "How Free One-Day Shipping Is Heating Up the Planet," CBS
    News, May 24, 2019, https://www.cbsnews.com/news/amazon-prime-
    day-one-day-shipping-has-a-huge-carbon-footprint/.

36 Lydia DePillis, "America's Addiction to Absurdly Fast Shipping Has a Hidden
    Cost," CNN, July 15, 2019, https://www.cnn.com/2019/07/15/
    business/fast-shipping-environmental-impact/index.html.

37 Syama Meagher, "The Not-So-Hidden Ethical Cost of Fast Fashion: Sneaky
    Sweatshops in Our Own Backyard," Forbes, February 5, 2020, https://
    www.forbes.com/sites/syamameagher/2020/02/05/the-not-so-
    hidden-ethical-cost-of-fast-fashion-sneaky-sweatshops-in-our-own-
    backyard/.

38 Xinran Y. Lehto et al., "Vacation and Family Functioning," Annals of Tourism
    Research 36, no. 3 (July 2009): 459–479.

39 Christian Montag and Jaak Panksepp, "Primary Emotional Systems and
    Personality: An Evolutionary Perspective," Frontiers in Psychology 8,
    (April 2017), article #464.

40 Cindy Chan and Cassie Mogilner, "Experiential Gifts Foster Stronger Social
    Relationships Than Material Gifts," Journal of Consumer Research 43,
    no. 6 (April 2017): 913-931.

41 Sharon Wheeler and Ken Green, "Parenting in Relation to Children's Sports
    Participation: Generational Changes and Potential Implications,"
    Leisure Studies 33, no. 3 (2014): 267-284.

42 KidsU. "How Can Extracurricular Activities Benefit My Child?" June 19, 2017.

43 Alvin Rosenfeld and Nicole Wise, The Over-Scheduled Child: Avoiding the
    Hyper-Parenting Trap (New York: St. Martin's Griffin, 2000).

44 Carly Dauch et al., "The Influence of the Number of Toys in the Environment
    on Toddlers' Play," Infant Behavior and Development 50, (February
    2018): 78–87.

45 Tracy Trautner, "Toys That Create High Quality Play," Michigan State University
    Extension, November 29, 2016, https://www.canr.msu.edu/news/
    toys_that_create_high_quality_play.

46 Eleanor Goldberg, "There's a Huge Problem with Kids' Toys That No One's

Talking About," Huffington Post, May 12, 2017, https://www.huffpost.com/entry/your-kids-toys-are-killing-the-planet_n_58ffa383e4b0f5463a1a9472.

47 Germaine M. Buck Louis et al., "Urinary Bisphenol A, Phthalates, and Couple Fecundity: The Longitudinal Investigation of Fertility and the Environment (LIFE) Study," Fertility and Sterility 101, no. 5 (February 2014): 1359–1366.

48 Ecology Center. "Adverse Health Effects of Plastic." https://ecologycenter.org/factsheets/plastichealtheffects/.

49 Yvette Brazier, "How Does Bisphenol A Affect Health?" Medical News Today, May 25, 2017, https://www.medicalnewstoday.com/articles/221205.

50 David J. Bredehoft et al., "Perceptions Attributed by Adults to Parental Overindulgence During Childhood," Journal of Family and Consumer Sciences Education 16, no. 2 (Fall/Winter 1998): 3–17.

51 Susan G. Groner, Parenting with Sanity and Joy: 101 Simple Strategies (Oakland: The Collective Book Studio, 2020), 50.

52 Dana Thomas, Fashionopolis: The Price of Fast Fashion and the Future of Clothes (New York: Penguin Press, 2019), 34.

53 Bethanie M. Carney Almroth et al., "Quantifying Shedding of Synthetic Fibers from Textiles; A Source of Microplastics Released into the Environment," Environmental Science and Pollution Research 25, no. 2 (January 2018): 1191-1199.

54 Kate Carter, "Pandering to the Green Consumer," The Guardian, August 12, 2008, https://www.theguardian.com/lifeandstyle/2008/aug/13/bamboo.fabric.

55 Paul Schneider, "The Cotton Brief," The New York Times, June 20, 1993, https://www.nytimes.com/1993/06/20/style/the-cotton-brief.html.

56 Kimberley Janeway, "Don't Bother Using Hot Water to Wash your Laundry," Consumer Reports, August 25, 2016, https://www.consumerreports.org/washing-machines/dont-bother-using-hot-water-to-wash-your-laundry/.

57 Helen Thompson, "The Case for Washing Clothes in Cold Water," Smithsonian Magazine, June 1, 2015, https://www.smithsonianmag.com/smart-news/case-washing-clothes-cold-water-180955459/.

58 n.d., "The Impact of a Cotton T-Shirt," World Wildlife Fund, January 16, 2013,

https://www.worldwildlife.org/stories/the-impact-of-a-cotton-t-shirt.

59 Lisa Anne Hamilton et al., Plastic & Climate: The Hidden Costs of a Plastic Planet, (Washington, DC: The Center of International Environmental Law, 2019), 8, https://www.ciel.org/wp-content/uploads/2019/05/Plastic-and-Climate-FINAL-2019.pdf.

60 Hamilton et al., Plastic & Climate, 4.

61 Robert Kunzig, "Is a World without Trash Possible?" National Geographic, February 18, 2020, https://www.nationalgeographic.com/magazine/2020/03/how-a-circular-economy-could-save-the-world-feature/.

62 Serm Murmson, "Plastic Recycling Symbols and Meanings in the USA," Sciencing, April 25, 2017, https://sciencing.com/plastic-recycling-symbols-meanings-usa-5977.html.

63 Melissa Pflugh Prescott et al., "Child Assessments of Vegetable Preferences and Cooking Self-Efficacy Show Predictive Validity with Targeted Diet Quality Measures," BMC Nutrition 5, no. 21 (March 2019).

64 Trevor Nace, "We're Now at a Million Plastic Bottles Per Minute—91% of Which Are Not Recycled," Forbes, July 26, 2017, https://www.forbes.com/sites/trevornace/2017/07/26/million-plastic-bottles-minute-91-not-recycled/.

65 Laura Parker, "How the Plastic Bottle Went from Miracle Container to Hated Garbage," National Geographic, August 23, 2019, https://www.nationalgeographic.com/environment/2019/08/plastic-bottles/.

66 Sergio Peçanha, "Congrats! You dump 100 plastic bottles in nature each year." The Washington Post. February 19, 2020.

67 Steven Kurutz, "Life Without Plastic is Possible. It's Just Very Hard," The New York Times, February 16, 2019, https://www.nytimes.com/2019/02/16/style/plastic-free-living.html.

68 Heidi Godman, "Pressed Coffee Is Going Mainstream—But Should You Drink it?" Harvard Health Blog, April 29, 2016, https://www.health.harvard.edu/blog/pressed-coffee-going-mainstream-drink-201604299530.

69 "Is Plastic a Threat To Your Health?" Harvard Health Publishing, December 2019, https://www.health.harvard.edu/staying-healthy/is-plastic-a-threat-to-your-health.

70 Hannah Ritchie, "Where In The World Do People Emit The Most CO2?" Our

World in Data, October 4, 2019, https://ourworldindata.org/per-capita-co2.

71 "Stove Versus Microwave: Which Uses Less Energy to Make Tea?" Scientific American, June 11, 2009, https://www.scientificamerican.com/article/stove-versus-microwave-energy-use/.

72 "Energy Saving Tips," Smarter House, accessed 2020, http://www.smarterhouse.org/cooking/energy-saving-tips.

73 "Energy Saving Tips."

74 Alexandra S. Richey et al., "Quantifying Renewable Groundwater Stress with GRACE," Water Resources Research 51, no. 7 (July 2015): 4861-5868.

75 Fiona Harvey, "Are We Running Out of Water?" The Guardian, June 18, 2018, https://www.theguardian.com/news/2018/jun/18/are-we-running-out-of-water.

76 Wilson Chapman, "10 Cities Most At Risk of Running Out of Water," US News, June 21, 2019, https://www.usnews.com/news/cities/slideshows/10-cities-most-at-risk-of-running-out-of-water.

77 Ben Simon, "What Environmental Problems Does Wasting Food Cause?" Forbes, July 18, 2018. https://www.forbes.com/sites/quora/2018/07/18/what-environmental-problems-does-wasting-food-cause/.

78 Dana Gunders, Wasted: How America Is Losing up to 40 Percent of Its Food from Farm to Fork to Landfill, (New York , NY: Natural Resources Defense Council, August 2012), https://www.nrdc.org/sites/default/files/wasted-food-IP.pdf.

79 Roger Harrabin, "Plant-Based Diet Can Fight Climate Change," BBC, August 8, 2019, https://www.bbc.com/news/science-environment-49238749.

80 Laura Parker, "Fast Facts About Plastic Pollution," National Geographic, December 20, 2018, https://www.nationalgeographic.com/news/2018/05/plastics-facts-infographics-ocean-pollution/.

81 "China Starts New Recycling Drive as Foreign Trash Ban Widens," Reuters, January 14, 2019, https://www.reuters.com/article/us-china-waste/china-starts-new-recycling-drive-as-foreign-trash-ban-widens-idUSKCN1P90A1.

82 Livia Albeck-Ripka, "Your Recycling Gets Recycled, Right? Maybe, or Maybe Not," The New York Times, May 29, 2018, https://www.nytimes.

com/2018/05/29/climate/recycling-landfills-plastic-papers.
html.

83 "National Overview: Facts and Figures on Materials, Wastes, and Recycling,"
United States Environmental Protection Agency, last modified 2017,
https://www.epa.gov/facts-and-figures-about-materials-waste-and-
recycling/national-overview-facts-and-figures-materials.

84 Sarah Spary, "National Recycling Week 2019: How Many Times Can One
Plastic Bottle Be Recycled?" Huffington Post, September 27, 2019,
https://www.huffingtonpost.co.uk/entry/how-many-times-
can-one-plastic-bottle-be-recycled_uk_5bc9b98be4b0d38b58771df3.

85 Simon Reddy, "Plastic Pollution Affects Sea Life Throughout the Ocean," PEW,
September 24, 2018, https://www.pewtrusts.org/en/research-
and-analysis/articles/2018/09/24/plastic-pollution-affects-sea-life-
throughout-the-ocean.

86 Joleah B. Lamb et al., "Plastic Waste Associated with Disease on Coral Reefs,"
Science 359, no. 6374 (January 2018): 460–462.

87 No Plastic in Nature: Assessing Plastic Ingestion from Nature to People,
(Gland, Switzerland: WWF International, 2019), https://   awsassets.
panda.org/downloads/plastic_ingestion_press_singles.pdf.

88 Tevere Macfadyen, "The Rise of the Supermarket," American Heritage,
October/November 1985, https://www.americanheritage.com/rise-
supermarket.

89 Alejandra Borunda, "Grocery Stores Are Packed with Plastic. Some
Are Changing." National Geographic, April 22, 2019, https://www.
nationalgeographic.com/environment/2019/04/plastic-
free-supermarket-grocery-shopping/.

90 n.a., "American Food Production Requires More Energy Thank You'd Think,"
Save On Energy, December 16, 2019, https://www.saveonenergy.
com/learning-center/post/american-food-production-requires-
energy/.

91 Michael Corkery, "A Giant Factory Rises to Make a Product Filling Up the
World: Plastic," The New York Times, August 12, 2019,
https://www.nytimes.com/2019/08/12/business/energy-environment/
plastics-shell-pennsylvania-plant.html.

92 National Geographic Resource Library, "Petroleum," https://www.
nationalgeographic.org/encyclopedia/petroleum/.

93 Fourth National Climate Assessment Vol. 2: Impacts, Risks, and Adaptation in the United States, (Washington, DC: US Global Change Research Program, 2018), 539-570, https://nca2018.globalchange.gov/downloads/NCA4_2018_FullReport.pdf.

94 Jon Hamilton, "Study: Most Plastics Leach Hormone-Like Chemicals," National Public Radio, March 2, 2011, https://www.npr.org/2011/03/02/134196209/study-most-plastics-leach-hormone-like-chemicals.

95 "Is Plastic a Threat to Your Health?"

96 Sarah Gibbens, "Exposed to Extreme Heat, Plastic Bottles May Ultimately Become Unsafe," National Geographic, July 19, 2019, https://www.nationalgeographic.com/environment/2019/07/exposed-to-extreme-heat-plastic-bottles-may-become-unsafe-over-time/.

97 Gibbens, "Exposed to Extreme Heat."

98 Leonardo Trasande, "Ask the Experts: Do the Plastic Linings of Tin Food Cans Contain BPA?" The Guardian, June 27, 2019, https://www.theguardian.com/us-news/2019/jun/27/tin-food-cans-linings-bpa-plastic-ask-experts.

99 Caroline Novas, "MyPlate: A New Alternative to the Food Pyramid," National Center for Health Research, accessed 2020, https://www.center4research.org/myplate-new-alternative-food-pyramid/.

100 Alejandra Borunda, "How Tampons and Pads Became So Unsustainable," National Geographic, September 6, 2019, https://www.nationalgeographic.com/environment/2019/09/how-tampons-pads-became-unsustainable-story-of-plastic/.

101 Richard Klasco, " Can a Bar of Soap Transmit Infection?" The New York Times, June 22, 2018, https://www.nytimes.com/2018/06/22/well/can-a-bar-of-soap-transmit-infection.html.

102 Sarah Gibbens, "A Brief History of How Plastic Straws Took Over the World," National Geographic, January 2, 2019, https://www.nationalgeographic.com/environment/2018/07/news-plastic-drinking-straw-history-ban/.

103 Donald Wuebbles, David W. Fahey, and Kathy A. Hibbard, "How Will Climate Change Affect the United States in Decades to Come?" Eos, November 3, 2017, https://eos.org/features/how-will-climate-change-affect-the-united-states-in-decades-to-come.

104 "Climate Effects on Health." Centers for Disease Control and Prevention, last
       modified August 21, 2020, https://www.cdc.gov/climateandhealth/
       effects/default.htm.

105 Alejandra Borunda, "Plunge in Carbon Emissions from Lockdowns Will Not
       Slow Climate Change," National Geographic, May 20, 2020, https://
       www.nationalgeographic.com/science/2020/05/plunge-
       in-carbon-emissions-lockdowns-will-not-slow-climate-change/.

106 The Nature Conservancy. "Calculate Your Carbon Footprint." Accessed
       October 2020. https://www.nature.org/en-us/get-involved/
       how-to-help/carbon-footprint-calculator/#:~:text=Globally%2C%20
       the%20average%20is%20closer,under%202%20tons%20by%202050.

107 Global Warming of 1.5 degrees Celsius. (Geneva, Switzerland:
       Intergovernmental Panel on Climate Change, 2018), https://www.ipcc.
       ch/sr15/.

108 "Public Transportation Is 10 Times Safer, Analysis Shows," Safety and Health
       Magazine, December 27, 2018, https://www.
       safetyandhealthmagazine.com/articles/17905-public-transportation-
       is-10-times-safer-for-commuters-analysis-shows.

109 Livia Albeck-Ripka, "How to Reduce your Carbon Footprint," The New York
       Times, accessed 2020, https://www.nytimes.com/guides/
       year-of-living-better/how-to-reduce-your-carbon-footprint.

110 Taylor Mabrey, "Reducing the Carbon Footprint? How Hybrid Cars Help the
       Planet." Choose Energy, accessed 2020, https://www.chooseenergy.
       com/news/article/how-hybrid-cars-help/.

111 Silvio Marcacci, "Charging an Electric Vehicle Is Far Cleaner than Driving
       on Gasoline, Everywhere in America," Forbes, March 14, 2018, https://
       www.forbes.com/sites/energyinnovation/2018/03/14/charging- an-
       electric-vehicle-is-far-cleaner-than-driving-on-gasoline-everywhere-in-
       america/.

112 Albeck-Ripka, "How to Reduce."

113 Tatiana Schlossberg, "Flying Is Bad for the Planet. You Can Help Make
       It Better," The New York Times, July 27, 2017, https://www.nytimes.
       com/2017/07/27/climate/airplane-pollution-global-warming.html?.

114 Julia Calderone, "The Truth About 'Reef-Safe' Sunscreen," Consumer Reports,
       February 7, 2019, https://www.consumerreports.org/sunscreens/the-
       truth-about-reef-safe-sunscreen/.

115 Livia Albeck-Ripka, "How to Reduce Your Carbon Footprint," The New York Times, n.d., https://www.nytimes.com/guides/year-of-living-better/how-to-reduce-your-carbon-footprint.

116 "Coca-Cola Produced More Than 110 Billion Plastic Bottles Last Year," EcoWatch, October 2, 2017, https://www.ecowatch.com/coca-cola-plastic-bottles-2492093659.html.

117 Blake Morgan, "Does E-Commerce Care About Sustainability?" Forbes, November 5, 2019, https://www.forbes.com/sites/blakemorgan/2019/11/05/does-e-commerce-care-about-sustainability/.

118 Shelagh McNally, "Is Online Shopping Really More Eco-Friendly?" Reader's Digest, August 27, 2018, https://www.readersdigest.ca/culture/is-online-shopping-really-more-eco-friendly/.

119 Melissa Allison and Monica Soto Ouchi, "Eco-Friendly Solvents Help Put "Clean" In Dry Cleaning," The Seattle Times, March 16, 2007, https://www.seattletimes.com/business/eco-friendly-solvents-help-put-clean-in-dry-cleaning/.

120 Public Health Statement for Tetrachloroethylene (PERC), (Atlanta: Agency for Toxic Substances and Disease Registry, 2019), https://www.atsdr.cdc.gov/phs/phs.asp?id=263&tid=48.

121 Mireya Navarro, "It May Market Organic Alternatives, but Is Your Cleaner Really Green? The New York Times, January 11, 2009, https://www.nytimes.com/2009/01/12/nyregion/12clean.html.

122 Navarro, "It May Market."

123 Marguerite Ward, "A Brief History of the 8-Hour Workday, Which Changed How Americans Work," CNBC, May 3, 2017, https://www.cnbc.com/2017/05/03/how-the-8-hour-workday-changed-how-americans-work.html.

124 Schools and Staffing Survey, (Washington, DC: National Center for Education Statistics, 2008), https://www.nces.ed.gov/surveys/sass/tables/sass0708_035_s1s.asp.

125 Oliver Burkeman, "This Column Will Change Your Life: How Long Does it Really Take to Change a Habit? The Guardian, October 9, 2009, https://www.theguardian.com/lifeandstyle/2009/oct/10/change-your-life-habit-28-day-rule.

126 Connor Simpson, "What It's Like to Work for a Nine-Year-Old in a Sweatshop,"
        The Atlantic, October 12, 2013, https://www.theatlantic.com/
        international/archive/2013/10/what-its-work-nine-year-old-
        sweatshop/310039.

127 D. J. Wuebbles et al., Climate Science Special Report (Washington, DC: US
        Global Change Research Program, 2017) 1–276.

128 "The Effects of Climate Change," Global Climate Change Vital Signs of the
        Planet, NASA, accessed 2020, https://climate.nasa.gov/effects/.

129 Lana Bandoim, "The Shocking Amount of Food US Households Waste
        Every Year," Forbes, January 26, 2020, https://www.forbes.com/sites/
        lanabandoim/2020/01/26/the-shocking-amount-of-food-
        us-households-waste-every-year/.

130 Neal Templin, "How Much Green Can Growing a Vegetable Garden Save
        You?" The Wall Street Journal, April 16, 2009, https://www.wsj.com/
        articles/SB123983924976823051.

131 Eliza Barclay, "Introducing Microgreens: Younger, and Maybe More
        Nutritious, Vegetables," National Public Radio, August 30, 2012,
        https://www.npr.org/sections/thesalt/2012/08/29/160274163/
        introducing-microgreens-younger-and-maybe-more-nutritious-
        vegetables.

132 Karen Russ, "Less Toxic Insecticides," Clemson University Home & Garden
        Information Center, last modified February 8 2019, https://hgic.
        clemson.edu/factsheet/less-toxic-insecticides/.

133 "The Science of Canning," America's Test Kitchen, April 13, 2016, https://
        www.americastestkitchen.com/articles/329-foolproof-preserving-the-
        science-of-canning.

134 Laura Parker, "We Made Plastic. We Depend on It. Now We're Drowning in
        It." National Geographic, June 2018, https://www.nationalgeographic.
        com/magazine/2018/06/plastic-planet-waste-pollution-trash-crisis/.

135 Lee Drutman, "How Corporate Lobbyists Conquered American
        Democracy," The Atlantic, April 20, 2015, https://www.theatlantic.com/
        business/archive/2015/04/how-corporate-lobbyists-
        conquered-american-democracy/390822/.

136 Richard Denison, "TSCA Reform Legislation: Enhancing EPA Testing
        Authority," Environmental Defense Fund Health Blog, April 15, 2015,
        http://blogs.edf.org/health/2015/04/15/tsca-reform-legislation-

enhancing-epa-testing-authority/.

137 Isabella Isaacs-Thomas, "Why Your Cosmetics Don't Have to be Tested for Safety," PBS, December 16, 2019, https://www.pbs.org/newshour/ health/why-your-cosmetics-dont-have-to-be-tested-for-safety.

138 "Introduction to Indoor Air Quality," United States Environmental Protection Agency, accessed 2020, https://www.epa.gov/indoor-air-quality-iaq/ introduction-indoor-air-quality.

139 Tara Parker-Pope, "Have I Been Cleaning All Wrong?" The New York Times, May 6, 2020, https://www.nytimes.com/2020/05/06/well/live/ coronavirus-cleaning-cleaners-disinfectants-home.html.

140 Lela Nargi and Danielle Braff, "What Kills Bacteria—And What Doesn't," Reader's Digest, September 12, 2020, https://www.rd.com/article/ what-kills-bacteria/.

141 Diamond Bridges, "Why You Should Never Use Oven Cleaner and What You Should Use Instead," MSN, March 23, 2020, http://www.msn.com/05/ en-us/BB11ByAp?ocid=st.

142 Jessie Sholl, "8 Hidden Toxins: What's Lurking in Your Cleaning Products?" Experience Life, October 2011, https://experiencelife.com/article/8- hidden-toxins-whats-lurking-in-your-cleaning-products/.

143 "'Greener' Laundry by the Load: Fabric Softener Versus Dryer Sheets," Scientific American, December 10, 2008, https://www. scientificamerican.com/article/greener-laundry/.

144 Robin E. Dodson et al., "Endocrine Disrupters and Asthma-Associated Chemicals in Consumer Products," Environmental Health Perspectives 120, no. 7 (July 2012): 935-943.

145 "Toxic Chemicals in Air Fresheners," Made Safe, January 19, 2020, https:// www.madesafe.org/toxic-chemicals-in-air-fresheners/.

146 "Personal Care Products Safety Act Would Improve Cosmetics Safety," The Environmental Working Group, accessed 2020, https://www.ewg.org/ Personal-Care-Products-Safety-Act-Would-Improve-Cosmetics-Safety.

147 Lauren Zanolli, "Pretty Hurts: Are Chemicals in Beauty Products Making Us Ill? The Guardian, May 23, 2019, https://www.theguardian.com/us- news/2019/may/23/are-chemicals-in-beauty-products-making-us-ill.

148 David O. Carpenter, Kathleen Arcaro, and David C. Spink, "Understanding the Human Health Effects of Chemical Mixtures," Environmental

Health Perspectives 110, no. 1 (February 2002): 25-42.

149 "Children Exposed to Daily Personal Care Products with Chemicals Not Found Safe for Kids," The Environmental Working Group, November 1, 2007, https://www.ewg.org/news/news-releases/2007/11/01/children-exposed-daily-personal-care-products-chemicals-not-found-safe.

150 Dodson et al., "Endocrine Disrupters."

151 Ioannis Tsialtas et al. "Neurotoxic Effects of Aluminum are Associated with its Interference with Estrogen Receptors Signaling," NeuroToxicology 77, (March 2020): 114–126.

152 P.D. Darbre. Journal of Inorganic Biochemistry. Volume 99, Issue 9, September 2005, Pages 1912-1919

153 Rebecca Adams, "Petroleum Jelly May Not Be as Harmless as You Think," Huffington Post, October 21, 2013, https://www.huffpost.com/entry/vaseline-petroleum-jelly_n_4136226.

154 Jonathan Watts, "The Environment in 2050: Flooded Cities, Forced Migration—and the Amazon Turning to Savannah," The Guardian, December 30, 2019, https://www.theguardian.com/environment/2019/dec/30/environment-2050-flooded-cities-forced-migration-amazon-turning-savannah.

155 Coral Davenport and Kendra Pierre-Louis, "US Climate Report Warns of Damaged Environment and Shrinking Economy," The New York Times, November 23, 2018, https://www.nytimes.com/2018/11/23/climate/us-climate-report.html.

156 Chunwu Zhu et al., "Carbon dioxide (CO2) Levels This Century Will Alter the Protein, Micronutrients, and Vitamin Content of Rice Grains with Potential Health Consequences for the Poorest Rice-Dependent Countries," Science Advances 4, no. 5 (May 2018).

157 Military Expert Panel Report: Sea Level Rise and the US Military's Mission, (Washington, DC: The Center for Climate and Security, September 2016), https://climateandsecurity.files.wordpress.com/2016/09/center-for-climate-and-security_military-expert-panel-report2.pdf.

158 Danae Lund, "Top 5 Benefits of Children Playing Outside," Sanford Health, June 26, 2018, https://news.sanfordhealth.org/childrens/play-outside/.

159 Claire McCarthy, "6 Reasons Children Need to Play Outside," Harvard Health
      Publishing, May 22, 2018, https://www.health.harvard.edu/blog/6-
      reasons-children-need-to-play-outside-2018052213880.

160 Christina Caron, "Risky Play Encourages Resilience," The New York Times, July
      21, 2020, https://www.nytimes.com/2020/07/21/parenting/risky-play.
      html.

161 Jason Plautz, "The Environmental Burden of Generation Z," The Washington
      Post, February 3, 2020, www.washingtonpost.com/
      magazine/2020/02/03/eco-anxiety-is-overwhelming-kids-wheres-line-
      between-education-alarmism/.

162 Anya Kamenetz, "How to Talk to Your Kids About Climate Change," National
      Public Radio, October 24, 2019, https://www.npr.
      org/2019/10/22/772266241/how-to-talk-to-your-kids-about-climate-
      change.

Mango Publishing, established in 2014, publishes an eclectic list of books by diverse authors—both new and established voices—on topics ranging from business, personal growth, women's empowerment, LGBTQ studies, health, and spirituality to history, popular culture, time management, decluttering, lifestyle, mental wellness, aging, and sustainable living. We were recently named 2019 *and* 2020's #1 fastest-growing independent publisher by *Publishers Weekly*. Our success is driven by our main goal, which is to publish high-quality books that will entertain readers as well as make a positive difference in their lives.

Our readers are our most important resource; we value your input, suggestions, and ideas. We'd love to hear from you—after all, we are publishing books for you!

Please stay in touch with us and follow us at:

Facebook: Mango Publishing
Twitter: @MangoPublishing
Instagram: @MangoPublishing
LinkedIn: Mango Publishing
Pinterest: Mango Publishing
Newsletter: MangoPublishingGroup.com/newsletter

Join us on Mango's journey to reinvent publishing, one book at a time.